Islamabad Travel Information Pakistan.

City Guide

Author
Carter White

Copyright Policy

Information-Source This Title is protected by Copyright Policy, any intention to reproduce, distribute and sales of this Title without the permission from the Title owner is strictly prohibited. Please when purchasing this Title, make sure that you obtain the necessary reference related to the purchase such as purchasing receipt. In accordance with this term, you are permitted to have access to this Title. Thanks for understanding and cooperation.

All-right reserved Information-Sourve
Copyright 2021..

Published
By
Information-Source.
16192 Coastal Highway Lewes,
DE 19958. USA.

Table of Content

ISLAMABAD.GUIDE... 1

INTRODUCTION 1
THE HISTORY... 7
TRAVEL GUIDE.. 12
   Health and Safety 19
   The charming capital 22
   Around Islamabad 32
      Murree Hills 33
      Taxila... 33
      Khanpur Dam 34
      Mughal Gardens 36
      Gurdawara Panja Sahib... 38
      Ayub National Park 38
      Khewra Salt Mines 40
      Kallar Kahar 42
      Katas Raj 43
      Rohtas Fort 44
      Mangla Dam 45
      Shinkiyari 46
      Kund.. 47
      Attock Fort 49
      Tarbela Dam... 50
      Chattar Park 51
      Lohi Bher Wild Life Park.. 51
   Things to Do... 52
      Margalla Hills 52
      Museums & Attractions 55
      Pakistan Monument Museum 57
      Shopping and Dining 59
         Shopping... 59
         Dining with a View.. 61
            Cheap Eats 63
         Locations 64
      Destinations 68
         Pakistan Monument: 69

    Shakarparian Hills: 69
    Daman-e-Koh: 70
    Buddhist Caves in Shah Allah Ditta: 70
    Buddhist Caves (Sadhu ka Bagh) 71
    Saidpur Village: 74
    Lok Virsa Cultural Center: 74
    Pothohari Arts and Crafts Village: 75
    Rose and Jasmine Garden: 76
    Margalla Hills National Park: 77
    Fatima Jinnah Park: 78
    Lake View Park: 78
    Murghzar Mini Zoo and Children Park: 79
Top Places to Visit in Islamabad 79
Quick Guide for New Travelers 89
  Understand 90

Islamabad.Guide
Introduction

Islamabad, the capital of Pakistan, is one of the most beautiful, green cities you will find in the country. Surrounded on one side by the lush green Margalla Hills, it gives a perfect blend of sightseeing and an urban lifestyle.

Being the capital, it is the most developed city in the country, and the most organized one. Areas are easy to access as the roads are well developed and mostly straight and at right angles to each other.

The city is divided into square areas of 4 km² each, called sectors. The sectors are arranged and numbered such that it is really easy to identify which direction a particular sector lies in. Each sector has a market or a shopping area in the middle, called the *Markaz*.

The usual way to commute is via taxi or cabs. Though one can rent a car from the various rent-a-cars operating here, or commute via the radio cabs which are just a phone call away.

Just adjacent to Islamabad lays the city of Rawalpindi, often simply called "Pindi." Interestingly, the Islamabad International Airport lies in Rawalpindi. However, the boundaries between the cities aren't discernible. You'll know when you enter the city because of the old houses and the congested roads. Rawalpindi also offers its decent share of visiting sites and delicacies.

The capital houses some prominent attractions. A 1-2 hour hike or 45-minute drive up the Margalla Hills takes you up Pir Sohawa, which offers a great view of the city, especially at night.

The place houses some prominent restaurants which specialize in local cuisine. Another prominent attraction is the Lake View Park located along the Kashmir Highway towards the Murree Hills. The park is built alongside the city's Rawal Dam. You can have a boating trip or jet ski in the reservoir. The Park also has the city's only Go Karting track, a café, and a paintball arena.

In the foot of Margalla Hills lies the Islamabad Zoo, the Playland (a children's park), and the Saidpur Village. The Saidpur Village was made into a model village by the administration, and offers a decent exposure to Pakistani rural life. There are a few decent restaurants and cafés here which serve local cuisine.

The Lok Virsa Museum located to Shakarparian Hills showcases cultures of different regions of the country, and is a decent place to shop for any souvenir items you may wish to take back. The road goes onto the Pakistan Monument which is a landmark worth seeing. The Pakistan Monument Museum also visually depicts the history of Pakistan through various times.

Pakistan is famous for its colorful and tasty food. You can find good restaurants in almost every sector; however, I would recommend the Tehzeeb Restaurant in F-8. Any caffeine cravings can be satisfied with a visit to any of the

Espresso Lounge, Coffee Planet, Coffee Republic, or Gloria Jean's Coffees outlets, other than almost every other café which serve coffee. The choice of drink here is tea, though, which is popularly available.

For shopping, the Centaurus Mall and the Safa Gold Mall are popular malls and host to most of the popular local and foreign brands. The F-7 Markaz is also a popular shopping market with almost all kinds of products available there.

A 1.5-hour drive along the Murree Road takes you to Murree, a hill station built in the days of the British rule here. You can enjoy the cool weather there, take a stroll along the mall road, or a further drive can take you to different *Galiyaats* each of which is a popular tourist resort.

These places are crammed in both the hottest as well as the coldest days as people look to spend time in a cooler setting, or want to enjoy a snowfall. A 1-hour drive along the famous Grand Trunk road takes you to Taxila, an ancient city with ruins found dating as back as the 6th century BC.

You can visit different sites of archaeological importance, the art and architecture from the days of Buddhist glory in the region. A 30-minute drive from Taxila takes you to the Khanpur Dam where you can enjoy archery, cliff diving, motor boating, fishing, and various other activities.

Overall, you will enjoy Islamabad's cleanliness and greenery, and the serene environment. For any visitors, Islamabad will probably be their first stop in Pakistan. Due to its location, the beautiful valleys of Kashmir, Gilgit, Naran, Kaghan etc, and the gigantic mountains to the north are easily accessible from Islamabad than other places. Be sure to include visiting the north in your trip plans, because that's where it gets the most beautiful.

There are many negative perceptions about the country, and the country has its fair share of problems, but visiting the country yourself will clear most negative opinions. The people are hospitable, the land is beautiful, and the culture is unique. Whether you are an adventurer, or a person seeking a spiritual journey, or someone who wants to travel the world; Pakistan has ample opportunities for everyone.

The History

The capital city of Pakistan, Islamabad is located in the northwest of the country on Potohar Plateau. This area has been significant in history for being a part of the crossroads of the Rawalpindi and the North West Frontier Province. The city was built in 1960 to replace Karachi as the Pakistani capital, which it has been since 1963. Due to Islamabad's proximity to Rawalpindi, they are considered sister cities.

Compared to other cities of the country, Islamabad is a clean, spacious and quiet city with lots of greeneries. The site of the city has a history going back to the earliest human habitations in Asia. This area has seen the first settlement of Aryans from Central Asia, ancient caravans passing from Central Asia, and the massive armies of Tamerlane and Alexander.

To the north of the city you will find the Margalla Hills. Hot summers, monsoon rains and cold winters with sparse snowfall in the hills almost summarize the climate of this area. Islamabad also has a rich wildlife ranging from wild boars to leopards.

After the formation of Pakistan in 1947, it was felt that a new and permanent Capital City had to be built to reflect the diversity of the Pakistani nation. It was considered pertinent to locate the new capital where it could be isolated from the business and commercial activity of the Karachi, and yet is easily accessible from the remotest corner of the country.

A commission was accordingly set in motion in 1958, entrusted with the task of selecting a suitable site for the new capital with a particular emphasis on location, climate, logistics and defense requirements, aesthetics, and scenic and natural beauty.

After extensive research, feasibility studies and a thorough review of various sites, the commission recommended the area North East of the historic garrison city of Rawalpindi. After the final decision of the National Cabinet, it was put into practice. A Greek firm, Doxiadis Associates devised a master plan based on a grid system, with its north facing the Margallah Hills. The long-term plan was that Islamabad would eventually encompass Rawalpindi entirely, stretching to the West of the historic Grand Trunk road.

Islamabad nestles against the backdrop of the Margallah Hills at the northern end of Potohar Plateau. Its climate is healthy, pollution free, plentiful in water resources and lush green. It is a modern and carefully planned city with wide roads and avenues, elegant public buildings and well-organized bazaars, markets, and shopping centers.

The city is divided into eight basic zones: Administrative, diplomatic enclave, residential areas, educational sectors, industrial sectors, commercial areas, and rural and green areas.

The metropolis of Islamabad today is the pulsating beat of Pakistan, resonating with the energy and strength of a growing, developing nation. It is a city, which symbolizes the hopes and dreams of a young and dynamic nation and espouses the values and codes of the generation that has brought it thus far. It is a city that welcomes and promotes modern ides, but at the same time recognizes and cherishes its traditional values and rich history.

Travel Guide

Islamabad is believed to be a piece of Art. While traveling to the City from the airport one can see the smooth transition from dirt, traffic and general unrest to greenery, the beautiful Hills and Majestic Faisal Mosque which catches your attention in a split second. The construction of the Islamabad began in 1960, but in about a decade the city had developed and emerged as one of the new national Capitals of the 20th century. Today the city has to boast a number of playgrounds, green belts, gardens, fountains, avenues, shopping centers, radio and TV headquarters, numerous newspapers, mulch-storied commercial and government buildings, a vast hospital complex, parliament building, Presidential palace, Prime Minister's Secretariat and his majestic residence, a sports complex, a zoo of sorts, and a vast city park .

The City was planned to perfection. The designer ensured that every sector had a public school, a mosque and some community centers. The class based division was not in the plan therefore all the large houses were connected to the smaller ones. The city turned out to be something completely different. A embodiment of the "elitist" society, the exploitation of our masses and the attitude of the people generally known to flaunt their superiority by claiming to be on top of the social class hierarchy. The twist in the plan of the city is very evident from how the entire map has been altered to the specifications of the Elite. The city discriminatory factor exists even in the most minute details, take the sectors for example. The design of the city caters to the economic standing of various classes and it keeps people from different financial prowess far away from each other.

Given the structure of the City, the mentality of the people is no different. Big business ti-cons, the politicians, feudal lords and the nouveau riche have all found it beneficial to have mansions in this part of the country to showcase their power and money. The 'money culture' is prevailing where everyone is in the line to make the most extravagant house or buy the most expensive car. The standard of living is set by the elite and the others are just blind followers. The general price level is known to be higher in Islamabad due to the "no bargaining" by the rich. The demand of everything is high, people are ready to pay whatever it takes to maintain their image. Likewise, the constant need to impress the other with help of showering money also persists. One is constantly under pressure by the actions of the "competitor".

This class is more prone to corruption given their constant desire to be better than the rest. There are cases of hypocrisy in terms of philanthropic motives. The auctions, the talks and the fundraising has also revolutionized. It not only about giving back to the society but has become a matter of self actualization. The wars of "who arranges the best fundraiser" prevails. The amount of money and time spent to prove to the society that one person can throw money around better than the other exists in Islamabad also just like any other class conscious society.

The term psychological barbie dolls fits the people living here perfectly. The culture having no limits on the credit cards is very commonly found. While, the men are busy managing the numerous businesses/investments/foul practices, the women indulge themselves in shopping sprees and throwing money around in cafes and restaurants. The children on the other hand are sent to privates school that are also ranked based on how much the parents are ready to pay. Sheikh zaed and Islamabad American being on top followed by Frobels and headstart moving down to The city school and Beaconhouse. The children also wear their ego on their arms roaming around like they own the place. Mostly neglected by their families, they find refuge in the company of similar boys and girls. Throwing parties, driving their parents' cars, smoking, drinking is all covered under the realms of the social status and are thought of being necessary to maintain their social standing.

The blame is not only on the people living in the city. The design seemed faulty from the beginning. The structure to only cater for the elite is prominent in its most important aspects. It is hard to find the boundary between with high and the low income residential areas, Islamabad is probably easily misunderstood as equal while it has been designed keeping in mind the grade structure. The Government workers are provided accommodation far away from their work place with no public transport system. The parks were strategically placed alongside the bureaucratic elite sectors while the other sectors were clearly neglected. In a city where the public graveyard has allotted areas (true for many graveyards in

Pakistan as well), the distinction between classes is extremely visible and the nature of the city's social atmosphere is abhorrent to anybody who seeks the promotion of social welfare. The very shape of the villages that are located within the 2km diameter from the downtown of Islamabad is a clear symbol of the City atmosphere and the way the elitist nature that has forced the welfare of the members of that particular class over the welfare of the poor in the City and throughout Pakistan.

The discrimination based of income classes leaves one speechless. The circulation of money and investment that has been accumulated only to favor the elite is the cause of the problem. by not building pointless hotel-residential-office complexes and actually trying to provide low-cost housing to the lower class who have been abandoned in shanty homes in the outskirts of the city can actually help in creating a better and equitable capital. By working on the public transport and increasing check and balance on the automobile sprawl can also be helpful. By increasing developmental projects in other sectors and not only focusing on the F and E sectors the standard of living can increase all together. By fixing these structural faults one can expect to use divide and rule to burst this elitist bubble.

Health and Safety

Islamabad can be a fairly safe place to visit. Having said this, there are certain precautions that should be taken in order to ensure a smooth trip through the capital city of Pakistan. Like always, common sense is the most important tool to be used in staying safe.

Pickpockets are not a major problem in Islamabad, but they have been known to hit unsuspecting tourists in certain areas. Be aware that the prime spots for pickpockets are crowded, public areas such as train and bus stations, as well as markets.

Demonstrations, protests and mass gatherings occur in major public areas. Avoid these situations as they can be dangerous.

There are certain diseases and illnesses that can be dangerous in Pakistan. Make sure to consult a doctor a few months before departing to ensure having gotten the proper vaccinations and immunizations.

Avoid walking alone at night (especially women). This is a general recommendation for any unfamiliar area, but should be followed in Islamabad as well. If staying with a group is not an option and walking is unavoidable, try to remain in lighted, public areas.

Dress for men and women should be conservative. No shorts or tank tops. Women should cover their arms and legs.

Special safety issue for women: Be careful. Expect men to cut in line in front of you. Don't protest You'll only cause yourself grief. Do not look anyone directly in the face when walking around. Look at the ground. Don't go expecting people to tolerate that you are a western woman and perhaps ignorant of their rules and don't even realize what you are doing is considered inappropriate for women. I had a few scary experiences. In private, people are very kind and expressive and lovely. But in public, generally expect to follow the rules. Islamabad is considered a religious center with a much smaller ratio of women to men, so intolerance of western women's ways is the norm. Pakistan is a very lovely country with mountains, forests, etc., as well as desert.

Do not drink water from the tap. Always drink bottled water.

The charming capital

Capital of Pakistan was shifted from Karachi to Islamabad in early 1960s because of Islamabad's central location in the country. The city was built to replace Karachi as a capital, Pakistan secretariat and government offices as well as houses for employees were built as no building was available here. In the beginning only government officers and a few businessmen were residing in Islamabad. The government officers' belonged to different parts of the country with the passage of time the population grew, also many people migrated from other countries and cities to Islamabad as of now its population has touched 15 lakhs.

When we talk about culture of Islamabad it doesn't have a unique culture of its own but when we look around we see a major chunk of migrants from different regions of Pakistan, Also foreigners are found residing here in many sectors of Islamabad with their own values and culture which in whole makes it a city with diverse culture and religions. People here are keen to adopt any new thing that comes in here and are very much inspired by the western culture. With time we see how their lifestyles are changing and molding according to the western culture.

Language

Our national language is Urdu. But people of Islamabad are more into speaking English and take less pride in using their own language. It has been observed that not being able to speak fluent English is now an embracement for many and they are judged on the basis of that. There exists a trend of using roman English for communication here that has unfortunately led to destruction of the original Urdu language. Other languages spoken in Islamabad include Punjabi, Pashto, Balochi and Pahari.

Food

Islamabad has been considered a dull city in terms of food and entertainment for many years but in past three to four years the trend of eating out has developed here and we see a wide variety of cuisines everywhere in Islamabad. There is no specific kind of food loved by the people of Islamabad as mentioned above the people here are from different regions and foreign countries so they keep trying new things and look up to anything that offers them a unique experience. Due to a huge number of foreigners residing here many foreign cuisines are witnessed as well and with time those cuisines have become popular among the people of Islamabad as they are attracted and inspired by the western culture and their food and lifestyles. We see many foreign food chains here i.e. KFC, Mcdonalds, Hardees, Cinnamon Café.

Also F-Sectors of Islamabad have now many new cuisines opening each day and are becoming very popular like Roasters, Street One café, Desperdes, Table talk, Andaaz etc. Basically 'Desi' food is loved by all and is cooked in households every day, we prefer oily and spicy food because that is what we are having since many years but people from different regions residing here have their own tastes and preferences but we generalize that all in the Desi category. So from Desi spicy Pakistani food e.g. Nihaari, paye, halwa poori, chapli kabab, BBQ etc to Italian Pizzas and pastas and American steaks and cocktails, all kinds of food and cuisines are loved by Islamabadis.

Entertainment
When it comes to entertainment we can call Islamabad an entertainment deprived city with

very few options for the people to go to. In the past few years we witnessed that many food chains opened up and unfortunately eating out is the only entertainment people have here. Many years back we did have a Navdeck cinema to go and watch movies other than eating out but that also closed down. The few entertainment facilities that we have now are the Lake view park rawal dam, F1 tracks that have recently developed, Rose and Jasmin Garden, Shakarpariyan, Lok Virsa museum, National Monument, Monal, Saidpur village Arena movie theatre that also came into existence a year ago and is mainly for the people residing in Bahria town, F-9 Park Mega zone and variety of restaurants. Centaurus mall is best place to go for shopping and fan. For all the other entertainment facilities people here have to move to Rawalpindi, Murree or northern areas. It will not be wrong if we call it the city of elites because majority here are the elites who can spend handsome amount on expensive outings and can afford to move out of the country for recreation facilities so are less bothered about the lack of entertainment facilities here. But for the middle class and lower class people there aren't many options to go to. The Shah Faisal Mosque in Islamabad is one of the biggest Mosque in the world.

Clothes

Despite Shalwar kamiz being the national dress of Pakistan, Islamabadis tend to follow whatever is the latest fashion all over the country and abroad. In the last couple of years different clothing brands have emerged taking style and fashion to a whole new level. This city of elites spends huge amounts of money on branded clothing because they can afford it for this reason we see many international brands now opening their outlets here. As mentioned above the inspiration with the western culture has resulted in majority now wearing western clothes i.e. short tops, jeans, Capris, sleeveless shirts etc. Whereas there is another side that keeps themselves fully covered with abayas, scarf and veil, so we cannot say there is a specific dressing followed over here. They wear what they feel suits their style. In my opinion it is all about how they want to carry themselves and affordability of course.

Sports

Islamabad has a multi-purpose Sports Complex opposite Aabpara. The complex includes Liaquat Gymnasium for indoor games, Mushaf Squash

Complex and Jinnah Stadium for outdoor games, which is a venue for regular national and international events. Islamabad has very talented and skills players; people here follow international football teams religiously. They love playing football and cricket but unfortunately because of lack of polishing and grooming of the talented players here we are not able to bring good players out of Islamabad.

Education and Health Care

Islamabad is a city of literate people; it has a literacy rate of 87% which makes it the highest amongst all the other cities of Pakistan. A large number of public and private sector educational institutes are present here. The higher education institutes in the capital are either federally chartered or administered by private organizations and almost all of them are recognized by the Higher Education Commission of Pakistan. Also high schools and colleges are either affiliated with the Federal Board of Intermediate and Secondary Education or with the UK universities education boards, O/A Levels, or IGCSE. So we see that quality education is available for people here. But education here is not affordable by all, any middle class person will not be able to afford the fees of quality institutions and unfortunately the government institutions are not delivering quality.

Being the capital of the country health services are available in abundance in different hospitals. It has both private and public medical centres. PIMS being the largest of all, followed by Shifa international, polyclinic, Kulsoom hospital, Ali medical, Al-maroof International, Capital hospital. People here are blessed to have good doctors here, but for fatal diseases like Cancer they have to move to other cities for better treatment facilities and health care equipments.

Law and Order
It being the capital law and order situation in here is good as compared to the other parts of the country where life and property is not safe. We can say that living conditions in Islamabad are good and people living in either parts of the country migrate to Islamabad to improve standard of living. All in all from every point of view Islamabad is the best city of Pakistan.

Around Islamabad

Once you are done with the tourist places in Islamabad, it is a good idea to move to the places which are around the city. The residents of the capital city can take a day trip or less to the following places, which without any doubt are worth seeing.

Murree Hills

The queen of Hills (Malka-i-Kohsar), Murree is hardly 50 Km from the federal capital of Pakistan. One can easily cover this distance in around an hour's time and enjoy cold breeze during summers and snow during winters. Besides Murree, one can also visit Nathia Gali, Ayubia, Khanspur, Bhurban, Patriata etc. Detailed account of these areas is given separately on this website.

Taxila

The second most visited destination in the vicinity of Islamabad is Taxila. The house of Gandhara Civilization is located only 30 KM on the North-West of Islamabad and it takes around 40 to 45 minutes to reach there. The best time to visit Taxila is winters or even March / April and October / November because one has to move a lot under sun in order to see archeological remains. In 1980, Taxila was declared a UNESCO World Heritage Site and in 2006 it was ranked as the top tourist destinations in Pakistan by 'The Guardian' newspaper. A visit to Islamabad is actually incomplete without visiting Taxila. Details about Taxila are also given separately on this website.

Khanpur Dam

Just 20 KM further ahead from Taxila towards Haripur is located Khanpur Dam. The dam is built on the Khanpur Lake, which originates from the water of Haro River. The dam, which is 51 meters high and can store approximately 110,000 acre feet of water, was primarily built to provide water for consumption and irrigations to different areas in the Punjab and Khyber-Pakhtunkuwa. However, the beautiful location of the dam provides the tourists with a natural recreational spot. The dam located with the exquisite Margalla hills on one side and beautiful blue waters on the other, catches the attraction of the visitors. This is one of the few areas in Pakistan where water sports facilities are available. Camel ride, boating, fishing and other water related adventures are the most common activities of the tourists. Private companies have invested by providing cliff jumping and diving lessons.

This dam/lake has been an active tourist area and many families visit the place for picnic. It is recommended that one should avoid visiting this area during hot days because there is hardly any shade. Besides, one cannot even enjoy eating fried fish during the summers. The fish restaurant, though do not provide very hygienic environment, yet are worth trying. During winter season, one can also enjoy the famous 'Khanpur Malta.' On the way there are many orange farms. People often purchase trees and thus kids could climb the trees and take oranges directly from the tree.

Those, who have some connections with the government sector, can also arrange for the beautiful guest house, situated on the top of the hill. It is place where one can even spend a couple of nights

Mughal Gardens

Mughal Gardens, constructed during the days of Akbar, are located in the city of Wah, which is less than an hour's drive from Islamabad. Akbar employed Ahmed Mehmar Lahori for the structural and architectural design of these gardens. These gardens are beautifully designed and have also been the foundation for many major architectural structures because of its clever and innovative design. The Department of Archeology has taken responsibility for the restoration of the main areas of the gardens. A team of researchers, in 2006, found evidence of modern water system at the foundation of these gardens. A person travelling on the Grand Trunk Road from Peshawar to Islamabad or one visiting Taxila and Khanpur Dam can halt for a while to see the historical gardens.

Gurdawara Panja Sahib

Gurdawara Panja Sahib, situated at Hasan Abdal around 50 KM from Islamabad, is one of the most sacred worship places for the Sikh community. The significance of the place is because of the presence of a rock believed to have the hand print of Guru Nanak imprinted on it. Twice a year, Sikhs visit this Gurdwara from all over the world. The Government of Pakistan can provide further facilities and develop the Gurdawara in a center of religious tourism. Even otherwise, the building of the Gurdawara is beautiful and is worth visiting. However, the compound is not open for the common people.

Ayub National Park

Ayub National Park or Ayub Park is historically known as 'Topi Rakh'. It is located some 4 KM from Rawalpindi zero point and thus is not more than half an hour's drive for the residents of Islamabad. This park is the largest national park of Pakistan and covers an area of about 2300 acres. Ayub Park is a very popular picnic point. A lot of attractions for both kids and adults are provided in the park

The park hosts Jungle Kingdom – an amusement park for kids with a rare collection of beautiful animals and birds, kept in open air areas. These areas are landscaped to the preferences of the species including lions, zebras, peacocks, swans and turkeys etc. There are a lot of very interesting rides for the kids and the grown-ups in the Jungle Kingdom. Besides this, Ayub Park also housed large gardens, a running lake with boating facility, an open air theatre and a garden restaurant. The park is also indigenous for rare botany and marine life. There is an aquarium which is home to a various rare fish and other marine life. The lake found in the park has water lilies and other various beautiful water plants. The park also includes a carving of all Pakistan's major leaders and heroes. It is a replica of Mount Rushmore, South Dakota in the United States.

Khewra Salt Mines

The world's second largest Salt Mines are located in Khewra near Pind Dadan Khan. Though it is about 200 KM from Islamabad, yet the fast moving motorway has reduced the distance to about two and a half hour. From the Lilla interchange on the Islamabad-Lahore motorway, a 30 KM metaled road leads to the oldest salt mines in Pakistan. Off late Pakistan

Railways has also started tourist trains to Khewra from both Lahore and Rawalpindi.

The presence of salt in the region was felt for the first time by Alexander's troops in about 320 BC. However, the real mines were discovered by Dr. H Warth, a mining engineer appointed by the British Rule, by developing an access tunnel to the ground level in 1872.

To enter the mines one has to go in a huge tunnel for which a train facility is also provided. Once inside the mine, one can feel salt all around him. Besides huge walls of salt, one can also see several ponds of salted water. However, the most attractive thing for tourists is the models of different places relevant to Pakistan and Islam, carved out by artists using salt. Sheesh Mahal, Minar-i-Pakistan and Mosque are a case in point.

The mines are one the most important things to be seen in Pakistan.

Kallar Kahar

Kallar Kahar is a tourist resort located at 140 KM from Islamabad right on the Islamabad – Lahore Motorway. This beautiful place is known for its natural gardens, peacocks and a fresh water lake. Takht-e-Barbi, a flat stage of stone, built by Mughal Empror Babar to address his army enhanced the importance of the resort. Babar admired the place where he halted on his way from Kabul to Delhi. He also planted a garden, Bagh-e-Safa, which still exists. There are also rides for kids on the bank of the lake. TDCP motel provides lunch and snacks. One can stopover for a break during a journey from

Islamabad to Lahore or vise-versa. A visitor to Khewra can also stop at the resort.

Katas Raj

Katas Raj, a temple situated in Katas village near Chakwal district, is a place of great religious importance for Hindu Dharam. This temple is as old as the days of Mahabharata and is dedicated to Lord Shiva. The smaller temples, built in pairs around the larger central temple, were built around 900 years or so ago. Hindus believe that bathing in the pond, at the foothill of the temple leads to the forgiveness of sins and helps attain salvation. The temple, however, is in a very bad shape and can only attract photographers who can capture the semi-ruined temples on the mount. Renovation of the temple, and facilitation of Hindu pilgrims could enhance religious tourism and helps Pakistan to earn foreign exchange.

Rohtas Fort

Rohtas fort, famous for its unique and beautiful architectural structure, is located near Jehlum, about 110 KM from Islamabad. This fort was built by Sher Shah Suri to protect the northern frontiers of his empire. The strong fortifications are built to withstand enemy attack and natural calamities. This fort is surrounded by massive walls which extend for more than 4 KM – these walls have gateways and bastions to attack on the enemy. Though the fort is not well maintained and a proper village is housed inside the walls of the fort, yet archeological remains provides temptation for the lovers of history and photography. The fortification wall, gates, Shahi mosque, Baolis and Rani Mahal are the major tourist attractions.

Mangla Dam

Mangla dam is located in Mirpur district of Azad Kashmir and is around 140 KM from Islamabad. It takes less than two hours to cover the distance. It is one of the two biggest dams in Pakistan. It was constructed in 1960s and still provides electricity to many areas of the country. The huge lake filled with deep blue water looks attractive to the eyes. However, due to major military establishment in the city many areas are restricted for the common public. Yet, in order to facilitate tourism, one side of the lake has been developed into a recreation area where facilities like boating, fishing and other water sports have been provided. The major attractions of the tourists are speed boats and water scooters. Besides this Mangla is also site of the historical Mangla Fort. Though a portion of the fort has been demolished during the construction of the dam, yet some of its portions are still accessible for the tourists. A person visiting Rohtas Fort can detour for half an hour and can also see Mangla Dam.

Shinkiyari

Some 160 KM from Islamabad on the Karakuram Highway lies an eye-catching picnic spot named Shinkiyari. Though, because of heavy traffic on the way, mainly between Abbotabad and Mansera, it sometimes take even four hours to cover the distance between Islamabad and Shinkiyari. Yet, because to the entertainment that Shinkiyari provides, a huge number of people, especially student trips, travel the distance from Islamabad and plan picnics there. The main attraction is Siran river with a water of not more than two to three feet and provides opportunity to play in the water even without knowing swimming. Crossing the hanging wooden bridge is another temptation of the tourists. Tourists also enjoy the cultivation of vegetable grains, sugarcane, tobacco leaves, rice and at the top of it tea in the sloppy fields around the location. One can further travel half an hour up hill to reach a relatively cold, hill spot covered with trees and water at Dadar.

Kund

Kund is a unique place where two rivers – River Indus and River Kabul meet. This junction can be seen from the main GT Road almost on the border between the Punjab and Khyber Pakhtunkha, i.e. the Attock Bridge. However, this place at a distance of about 120 KM from Islamabad can best be reached by using Islamabad – Peshawar Motorway. One needs to get off from the motorway at Swabi exit and then take Swabi-Jahangiria road to reach the destination. Previously, the tourist could only see the meeting of the two colours water from the road but now the place has been turned into a major recreational area. People from the surrounding areas such as Islamabad, Attock, Mardan etc. visit the place for picnic and spend the entire day there. An amusement park, which hosts many activities for the tourists including boating, fishing, rides for kids, areas for playing sports and dining, adds importance to this scenic location. Eating fresh fried fish on the bank of the river is an old tradition of the tourists visiting the area.

Attock Fort

Attock Fort is another important historical monument located on the back of river Indus at the border town between the Punjab and Khyber Pakhtunkha. There are contradicting versions about the construction of the fort. According to one school of thought it was built by the Mughal emperor Akbar while the others consider Nadir Shah as the one who constructed it. However, this is for sure that the fort featured a prominent role during Sikh – Afghan wars. The beautiful red brick construction and the scenic location of the fort, makes it look beautiful. Off late the fort is under the military control and thus prohibited for the tourists. Yet, it is advisable for those who visit Kund or are travelling from Islamabad to Peshawar by GT Road to enjoy at least the distant view of this attractive historical monument.

Tarbela Dam

World's largest earth filled dam, Tarbela Dam is located in Khyber Pakhtunkhuwa, 130 KM from Islamabad. However, because of the motorway, it takes less than two hours to cover the distance. The dam forms the Tarbela reservoir with a surface area of approximately 250-square KM. The dam was completed in 1974 and was designed to store water for irrigation, flood control and the generation of hydroelectric power. It provides for a beautiful scenic location. Recently, the Government of Pakistan has decided to develop recreational and theme parks to promote tourism on this spot of natural beauty. It is planned to construct water sports points, restaurants and water jetty.

Chattar Park

18 KM from Islamabad on the way to Murree lies Chattar park. In the old days Chattar was known only for the loquat gardens and water stream. However, now an amusement park has been constructed and many families with children travel less than half an hour in the evening to enjoy the rides. There are also some eating places and some stalls of handicraft and other items attracting mainly women. 6 KM from Chattar, on the same Islamabad – Murree road is another amusement park at Salgiran.

Lohi Bher Wild Life Park

Located just off the main Islamabad highway, some 15 KM from zero point is the Lohi Bher Wild Life Park. Though the park is not of international standards, yet the main attraction is the Lion House. In a huge compound with natural jungle environment more than four lions are kept. One can drive in the area and see the lions in pure safari atmosphere. Besides lions there are many other animals and birds mainly kept in natural setting.

Things to Do
Margalla Hills
Inside Beautiful Margallah Hills

Beautiful Green Margallah Hills, sourrounding Islamabad from 2 sides, is a branch of Himalyan Mountains Series and. These are also in Frontier province including the areas of Haripur Hazara in the North-west of Islamabad. This series also includes the famous historical city of Taxila in west of Islamabad , and also connects to the Muree Hills and PirPanjar Hills which are further connected to Kashmir mountain areas (towards the East of Islamabad).

Margallah Hills under clouds, in Rain

These mountains are very famous among the people of Pakistan , especially people of twin cities, Islamabd and Rawalpindi . For hikers, there are very beautiful places in these hills. There are many small and large villages in the moutains, most famous are PirSohawa, which is also a famous picnic spot and hill station, Gokina is the village, which is in the Hiking treck towards PirSohawa.

A small road which is a walking treck at PirSohawa

A famous picnic spot called "Daman-e-Koh" (means, in between the mountains) is an attractive place for those who just want to enjoy picnic, eating and tea etc. It is now developed by government in much better shape along with the facilities like small cars to take you to View point and hotel from your Parking. BTW, the ride of these busses is a nice experience.

I'm sorry, I don't have any picture of these, but you can check for Daman-e-Koh hill point from:

People used to hike not just for fun, but also for exercise and so, there are some trails which are famous for such activity. Trail 3 is the famous one, which is used by hikers and exercisers to enter into Margallah Hills.

View from Islamabad City

If you observe Margallah Hills from Islamabad, you will notice that Margallah Hills series start gaining height from West of Islamabad and reaches to heigh altitudes in the North-East direction (as far I estimated the direction). In fact, in NorthEast, it touches Muree Hills, which are on big heights are famous for their cool environments.

Views from Margallh Hills

From many points in Maragallah Hills, you can observe many beautiful views of Islamabad city and Margallah Hills itself. As you go deep into the margallah hills, you will find more beauty.

Museums & Attractions

There are numerous cultural attractions that can be found in and around the city of Islamabad , which include various museums, a number of mosques and shrines, historical monuments, parks, art galleries and more.

The Pakistan Museum of Natural History displays the early history of the area today known as Pakistan , through a wide range of exhibits. Located in the National Park on Garden Avenue , it is perfectly situated to show how the geology of the land has developed over the centuries. Wildlife and the early humans are also portrayed in the museum. Admission is free to all, and the hours of operation are 9am to 4pm every day of the week, except on Fridays when it is closed.

The Faisal Mosque is one of the most famous religious sights in the city of Islamabad , and is one of the largest mosques in the entire world. The construction of the mosque began in the 1970's, and took a decade to finish. The mosque opened to the public in 1986, and was used by the Islamic University.

Pakistan Monument Museum

Pakistan Museum of Natural History is located at Garden Avenue Shakarparian, short of Lok Virsa on the left side of the road once you are moving to Lok Virsa or National Monument. It remains CLOSED on FRIDAY. For rest of the days it is open from 10:00 AM to 5:00 PM. It has a very nominal entrance fee is about Rs: 10 per individual and free for students.

At the entrance you will see a very large skeleton of Blue Whale which was found at Pasni (Balochistan) in 1967.

Inside the Museum there are five major display galleries

First is Biological gallery which displays the wild flora and fauna portrayed in their respective habitats. Second is the Ecological gallery; an educational section where ecological cycles, habitats and environmental problems are seen through visuals and audios. Third is Gemstones gallery which shows a variety of gems in raw as well as in cut and polished forms. Fourth is the Palaeontology gallery which displays fossils along with their studies. Anthropology is also discussed through paintings and writings including a skull of Astralopithecus. Wall paintings depict the pre-historic era. Fifth is the Tethys gallery which provides information about oceanology, petrology, pedology and mineralogy of Pakistan. It displays three-dimensional diorama of seascapes as well as a skeleton of a whale. Different aspects of Salt Range are also depicted in detail.

A must see place for Natural History Lovers and kids of all ages.

Shopping and Dining

Shopping
Well I grew up in the twin cities of rawalpindi and Islamabad. Islamabad is one of the beautiful cities in the world. Its quite lush green. There are many places to visit in Islamabad. If you are into shopping and would love to take some souveniers home then don't miss Jinnah super market. It has an excellent leather shop called traditions where you can easily get a great quality leather wallet for under $15. They ahave other good leather stuff too like ladies purses

and office stationary item and the best thing is they can personalize anything. If you roam around a little in Jinnah super you will find some really cool hadicraft shops too but they might be a little expensive but in Pakistan most of the shopkeepers bargain so u can offer a price and if they except it, its yours.

In hadicrafts shops you can find some hand embroided cushion covers or stoles, shawls, bed spreads some kurtas, sometimes traditional shoes too. I think a good hadicraft shop is in Super market which is about 2 km from Jinah super market. The super market has a shop called Threadline Gallery which has a very good variety of all the crafts done in Pakistan. Most of the things are handmade and you can even find carpets at a good price. In super market there are some good eatries like a place called munchies where u can grab some traditional pakistani snack food like samosas, Chana chat, Gol gapay or even some burgers with minch meat patties.

Public transportation is a little difficult to travel in so It would be advisable to rent a car which is pretty cheap and easier to travel in . Rest is good. I am sure you will enjoy your trip

Dining with a View
If you would like to experience the beauty of the northern areas while remaining in the vicinity of the capital, then the Margalla hills is the place to be. Just grab a car (rent it or just hire a radio cab) and start your journey. Just a mile up is daman-e-koh. It offers magnificent food in a calm, green environment with a mind-blowing view.

If you would like a better experience and have a little more time then travelling a little more to peer-sohawa should cannot and shouldnot be missed out. the road snaking its way through the margalla hills offers a comfortable and a safe journey with a breathtaking view all along (avoid travelling late night like after 11 pm). There's a restaurant called 'monal' there. The food is awesome with a impressive view too. With live music and a desi (traditional) touch you will defenitely love it. And most importantly don't forget to do sheesha after your meal. (Sheesha is an arabian styled hooka, just ask them for it and they'll expalin what it is. Although its not very harmful but kids under 18 aren't allowed to do it).

If you're afraid of heights, then going to have ice cream or coffee at Hotspot (sector f-6 near

Marriot hotel) is another place offering a serene and romantic environment.

Cheap Eats

In supermarkets there are some good eateries, like a place called Munchies where you can grab some traditional Pakistani snack food like samosas, chana chat, gol gapay or even some burgers with minch meat patties.

When eating in Islamabad, don't miss the Food Park -it's near Melody in Abpara. The food park has lots and lots of options. It's just like a food court where you have lots of small shops, and you get a table and the waiter brings you all the menus and you select what things you want to eat from which place. One thing not to miss there is Bihari Kebabs with Parathas from Rajput. They are a little spicy but the meat is so tender that it just melts in your mouth.

Locations

<u>Jinnah Super:</u>

Jinnah Super Market situated within the heart of the city, sector F-7, has become the most recognized and iconic shopping areas of Islamabad. It hosts a huge number of shops, restaurants, casual dining areas, and a whole lot more. There are the trendiest designer shops, cafes, eateries, banks, bookstores, gift and CD shops and service facilities. All in all, a visit to Jinnah Super, or "Jinnah" as it is endearingly referred to is unavoidable during a visit to Islamabad.

<u>Aabpara:</u>

Located close to the center of the city, Aabpaara is the oldest and most comprehensive market in Islamabad. It is also the one market in the capital city that has the greatest variety, where one can find almost anything. There are dry fruit stores, antique toy shops, novelty shoe stores, mechanical and electrical repair kiosks, clothes, consumer electronics and a wealth of so much more with everything at a very reasonable, affordable price.

Super Market:
Similar to Jinnah Super, Super Market is also a haven for the trendy and hip. A much larger and older market, this precinct has a lot more variety than other markets, and houses some very novel and exotic stores. Apart from the everyday books, clothes, shoes and movie stores, Super Market has Islamabad's oldest and best chemists, opticians, sports stores, photographer?s studio, bakery and an entire nook dedicated to the culinary arts.

Karachi Company/ G-9 Markaz:

Named after traders who had settled from Karachi in order to start a business, this market is remarkable in every sense of the word. There is a whole range of consumer items available here, at the best prices, everything from small jewellery to the largest household goods. Of particular mention are the diverse food items, since it is an Afghan population center, giving it a typically Middle Eastern atmosphere.

Melody Market:
Close to the Aabpaara Market is the Melody Market, known throughout the city for its excellent clothing and accessory stores, food joints and novelty bookstores. The market is also one of the oldest in the city, and because of its affordability and easy prices; it attracts a throng of people from all walks of life. Islamabad's most convenient and accessible shopping area.

Blue Area:

The commercial hub of the city, and technically the "Central Business District" of Islamabad, Blue Area stretches across a range of more than 2 kilometers. The area contains shops and businesses of all kinds, from doctor's clinics to laboratories, to eateries and novelty electronics items. Definitely worth a visit when in Islamabad.

Peshawar More:

A hawker's paradise, and home to countless small, cluttered shops, Peshawar More is teeming with bustling hardware stores, little restaurants and snack bars and a lively atmosphere. Located at the crossroads of G-9 and G-8, the area is also within walking distance to the famed Sunday bazaar, another place full of kiosks and stalls brimming with wares of all kinds.

F-10 Markaz:
The F-10 Markaz is one of the oldest market places in the city, and has grown exponentially through the time-phases of the development of Islamabad. The area has a wide range of commercial activity, from large restaurants, to burger stalls, video libraries and clothing stores.

G-8 Markaz:
The G-8 Markaz, also one of the oldest markets in the city has a speciality unlike any other in the city: a huge second-hand automobiles market. The market contains vehicles ranging from the latest model sports cars to old antiquated Volkwagens and 1940s era Willys jeeps. For car enthusiasts, definitely a place worth nosing around in.

Destinations

Pakistan Monument:

Pakistan Monument in Islamabad, is a national monument representing the nation's four provinces and three territories.

The Monument has been designed to reflect the culture and civilization of the country and depicts the story of the Pakistan Movement, dedicated to those who sacrificed themselves for future generations. From air the monument looks like a star (center) and a crescent moon (formed by walls forming the petals), these represent the star and crescent on Pakistan's flag.

Shakarparian Hills:

The historic Shakarparian Hills is famous for the trees planted by varipous Heads of State. The beautiful park with its central fountain and panoramic view of the whole city from vintage point at a height of 609 metres, is one of islamabad's favourite recreation spots.

Daman-e-Koh:

The area has now developed intot the most popular recreation and picnic spot of Islamabad. Daman-e-Koh offers spectacular views of the entire city, especially by night. Translated as 'Heart of the Hill', Daman-e-Koh has recently been terraced, and to avoid the rush of vehicles, has just introduced Golf Carts to carry visitors from the parking area to the viewpoint. A number of high quality restaurants and eateries have opened up, offering some sumptuous cuisine to travel-weary visitors.

Buddhist Caves in Shah Allah Ditta:

Shah Allah Ditta is a centuries-old village and a union council located at the foothills of the Margalla Hills in the Islamabad Capital territory. The Village is believed to be more than seven hundred years old and was used as route from Kabul to Gandharan City of Taxila by Alexander and Sher Shah Suri while Mughal rulers and other emperors often passed through while traveling from Afghanistan to the Hindustan. Relics of the Buddhist era dating back to the 8th century can be found here along with burnt diyas and trees with amulets tied to them. Shah Allah Ditta caves are located on the route leading towards Khanpur. These caves are next to the shrine and tomb of Shah Allah Ditta.

Buddhist Caves (Sadhu ka Bagh)
The Buddhist caves of Shah Allah Ditta (also known as the Sadhu ka Bagh) and the Losar

Baoli, or Stepwell, nearby way up in the Margalla Hills. These sites, though minor, present a pleasant small cluster of things to see, as well as a peaceful spot for a quiet picnic. The caves of Shah Allah Ditta are said to date to the Buddhist period, and include remnants of Buddhist-era murals. We did not see any such remnants, but the small chambers carved out of the hillside, and the clear spring flowing out, suggest ancient human habitation. 2,400-year-old Buddhist era murals of Buddha appear on the walls of caves at Shah Allah Ditta.

Archaeological evidence indicates that the caves and the platform-like formations surrounding the area were first used for meditation by Buddhist monks and later by Hindu sadhus before Muslim ascetics took over during the Mughal period. Marked on the ground close to the caves the location where Alexander arrived and was received by Raja Ambi, King of Taxila. The road next to the caves that leads to the main top of the mountain, Shah Allah Ditta road, is said to be built on the exact path followed by Pashtun emperor Sher Shah Suri during his visit. Moving up the mountain from the caves, there is a stepwell called Losar Baoli and a mosque built by Shahab-ud-Din Ghori. The mosque has broken walls and the road leading to it is dilapidated.

This village is surrounded by the great Margalla hills which increase the beauty of this area. This village represent many historical things and places like caves etc. It is said that once this place was the patch of Sher Shah Suri the lion of Afghanistan and construction of Rohtas Fort Jhelum. He also built the Gernaly Sarak (General's road) on this village; few parts of this road are still visible and tell us the glory. This road was used to travel from India to Afghanistan; and old wall of this road is still present in its original condition. This is a wall with 90 feet length and 2 and half feet width. The height of this wall is approximately 30 feet from the ground. The hard stones were used in its construction and it is still in its original condition.

Saidpur Village:
Situated to the East of Damn-e-Koh and reached by a leading North from the top end of F-6, this small village, surrounded by mango trees, is a centre of traditional pottery wares. Before partition, it was predominantly Hindu, and the springs in the areas were considered holy.

Lok Virsa Cultural Center:

Sprawled across a huge area, the Lok Virsa (National Institute of Folk and Traditional Heritage) works towards preserving the folk (traditional) culture of Pakistan. It houses artistes, craftsmen, artisans and musicians coming from across the country. The Folk Heritage Museum, located near Shakarparian Hills, has on display a large variety of embroidered costumes, jewelry, woodwork, metalwork, block printing, ivory and bone work in addition to the different stages of history that this region has passed through.

Pothohari Arts and Crafts Village:
The "Potohari" Arts & Craft Village has been constructed on 26 acres of area with the view to promote the indigenous arts and handicrafts and to enhance the inter-provincial harmony.
The Arts & Crafts Village is equipped with

exhibition hall, clusters of shops, studios for the artists, tea shops, show rooms, folk theatre and hostel for the visiting artisans.

The Arts & Craft village is providing an opportunity to the artisans and artists not only from the different area of country but also serving as a hub of cultural activities for the South Asian Region.

Rose and Jasmine Garden:
A picturesque garden, specifically for the purpose of growing a multitude of varieties of rose and jasmine, this 20,360 sq. meters garden is a picture of serenity. It contains more than 250 different varieties of roses, as well as more than ten different types of Jasmine. Seasonal flower shows are occasionally held here, particularly during spring.

Margalla Hills National Park:

Pakistan is home to some exotic flora and fauna in the Indian sub continent. The wildlife sanctuaries and national parks in Pakistan offer some exciting wildlife tour options. If you are in Islamabad, a wildlife tour to Margalla Hills National Park is a must. The Margalla Hills National Park is situated in the foothills of the Himalayas and is one of the easily accessible national parks in Pakistan.

The Margalla Hills are a series of hills located north of Islamabad, Pakistan. The Margallas are excellent for hiking purposes and cater to both the serious hiker and the less serious enthusiast. The best seasons to hike are the mild winter months when there is less rain and the days are extremely pleasant. The Margalla Hills National Park is home to a number of wild animals that include barking deer, wild boars, Asiatic leopard, chinkara, red fox, leopard and jackals.

Fatima Jinnah Park:
The largest park, in terms of area, in the whole of Asia, Fatima Jinnah Park is a sprawled scenic wonderland. It has a walking and jogging track, where people from all across the city come for some peaceful calm. In addition to several hundred acres of green wilderness, Fatima Jinnah Park is also undergoing uplifting and development.

Lake View Park:
At the base of Daman-e-Koh is located the Marghazar Mini Zoo and the Children's "Japanese Park". The zoo itself is small and has undergone rehabilitation, yet its fascinating array of animals never fails to entertain. The

Children Japanese Park, a gift from the Japanese Government, is also interesting with minimalist swings made of bamboo wood.

Murghzar Mini Zoo and Children Park:
At the base of Daman-e-Koh is located the Marghazar Mini Zoo and the Children's "Japanese Park". The zoo itself is small and has undergone rehabilitation, yet its fascinating array of animals never fails to entertain. The Children Japanese Park, a gift from the Japanese Government, is also interesting with minimalist swings made of bamboo wood.

Top Places to Visit in Islamabad

Creating beauty and preserving cultural heritage are goals for any assiduous urban planner, and few capitals around the globe can kill two birds with one stone, juxtaposing the old and the new with spectacular neck-craning wonders. Pakistan's capital city of Islamabad however has some legitimate swagger to boast about. Stunning pyramidal mosques share the green cityscape, dotted with relaxing and family-friendly parks, rustic ruins, and avant-garde markets for the youthful hip crowd. Its no wonder that Pakistan's pride gets on the podium for being the 2nd most beautiful city in the world, an often overlooked prestige that many people are oblivious to.

Cultural Heritage Sights

For many fresh-off the plane travelers, the absence of skyscrapers and electric-flashing districts should be a sight of relief. Islamabad's historical sites not only chronicle Pakistan's development as a nation since it's formation in

1947, but offer unique insight into the cultural diversity of Pakistani people.

1) The Pakistan Monument.
Nestled in the Shakarparian forest-covered hills overlooking the city, the Pakistan Monument stands erect as a petal-closed flower, arching its pointed granite blocks together towards the sky just as sports players embrace each other before a game. This harmonic convergence symbolizes Pakistan's national unification and solidarity as one people.

In addition, the four converging petals represent Pakistan's major provinces – Balochistan, Punjab, Kyhber-Pakhtunkwa and Sindh while the shorter petals sandwiched between them portray Pakistan's territories – specifically Azad Kashmir, GilgitBaltistan, and government controlled Tribal Areas.

Ensconced on top of a patio foundation made up of marble, the patriotic structure allow's a picturesque bird-like view of the capital. The national monument also offers an exquisite wax statue exhibit, depicting the country's arduous endeavor in winning independence and founding a new nation.

2) LokVirsa Museum
Five minutes by foot from Pakistani's monument, the LokVirsa museum, meaning "place of people's heritage," is another beautiful exhibit illustrating the unique culture of Pakistani people. Working in collaboration with UNESCO, the museum owes its outstanding maintenance and well-preserved artifacts to the organization's donations.

Displaying pieces of pottery, art, musical instruments, religious statues, and architectural relics the museum takes you on a pleasant walk through an outside garden while escorting you through nine galleries of Buddhist and Sufi shrines dating back to antiquity.

3) Faisal Mosque
Recognized as one the most iconic structures of Islamabad in travel photography, the desert-tented mosque holds one of Islam's most divine places of worship as it stretches above a surface area of 5000 square meters. Flanked with four towering spires on each corner, the sacred temple stands as an illuminated beacon from any vantage point across the city.

Accommodating nearly a quarter million people to worship, the modern-looking wonder is situated at the foundation of the Margalla hills. Intricately carved mosaics of marble and glass in triangular patterns hang from the tented ceiling in the prayer room which itself can hold over 10,000 people. Adjacent to the prayer room is the primary lecture hall as well as a library, restaurant and a cafe.

4) Saidpur Village
If your're looking for a rustic down-to-earth break from Islamabad's glitzy malls and teeming bazaars, Saidpur village is a great place to experience authentic village life in a 21st century metropolis. Meandering through the square-roofed village in a ravine of the Margalla hills, one can visit a Hindu temple and a Sikh gurdwara.

Feel free to roam the laid-back gravelly streets as children run and greet and you around the ancient artwork and residents playing sitaars enjoy the town's simple and traditional lifestyle.

High quality restaurants such as *Des Pardes* and *DeraPakhtoon* will give you some sizzling plates of spicy chicken masala as you gaze upon the Himalaya foothills.

Natural Attractions

Sometimes nicknamed the "Green City," Islamabad is famous for its nature-loving residents and scenic attractions.

5) Margalla hills and Daman-e-Koh Park

The hilly forest-covered terrain of the Margalla range leading up to the Himalaya mountains is visible around Islamabad and is often traversed by vista-seeking enthusiasts.

Walking up the trails you may see some of the range's abundant wildlife such as the Rhesus macaque monkey and the Asian Paradise flycatcher, a rare and exotic bird with a long light-grayish tail.

Meaning "foot hills" in ancient Persian language, Daman-e-Koh is a spectacular vista point in the Margalla hills where one can get a panoramic view of Islamabad and the picturesque Faisal mosque on the horizon.

6) Rawal Lake
Flowing down from the Margalla hills, the Korang river pours into the Rawal lake, a scenic reservoir in the Malpur village district of Islamabad. Interlaced around its perimeter are gardens with picnic spots under shady groves and quiet paths to saunter with loved ones. Taking paddle and motor boats out on the lake are great activities for families and friends.

Food and Nightlife

Taking it to the streets in Islamabad's active yet tolerable nightlife scene is an adventurous way to meet friendly locals over some delicious Pakistani cuisine.

7) Monal Restaurant
Located in Daman-e-Kohpark, this high quality and affordable restaurant specializes in chicken and rice dishes ranging from chicken Seekh kebabs to Biryani South Asian rice. The restaurant is ranked as the number one eating-out joint in Islamabad and the view over the city is irresistible.

8) Islamabad Club
If you're hoping to get some rest and recreation and plan to stay in Islamabad for a while, becoming a member at the chic Islamabad club is a relaxing way to enjoy leisure activities –

including swimming, playing tennis, and reading books.

Touted as one of the elitist hangout spots for ministry of government officials and foreign diplomats, the club offers a fusion style buffet of world cuisine with sumptuous hotel-like suites.

9) Jinnah Supermarket
Famous as a trendy hang out spot for youth and fashion-seekers, this circular shaped supermarket complex offers a smorgasbord of world dishes, cafes, hole-in-the wall eateries and music stores.

10) Itwar Bazaar
Last but not least on the endless things to do in Islamabad is shopping at the Sunday market. Teeming with a grand assortment of cheap second-hand goods, fresh fruits and vegetables,

and odds and ends the market opens its doors on Sundays as well as on Tuesdays and Fridays.

Islamabad is a gorgeous city with a diverse array of interesting places to visit and food to savor, and venturing to Pakistan's heartland will leave with you with very fond memories

Quick Guide for New Travelers

Islamabad has been the capital of Pakistan since 1963. The name of the city is derived from two words, Islam and abaad, meaning "City of Islam" or "Abode of Islam". Islam is an Arabic word which refers to the Faith of Islam with many forms of variations of the Abrahamic Religion and -abad is a Persian place name that means inhabited place or city. The original name of the city is Ramakund which refers to the Hindu temples and holy lakes that once populated the region.

Understand

Although the majority of the population in Islamabad traditionally have been employees of the Federal Government, the wealth of the Musharraf years fuelled a boom and it is becoming an important financial and business city. In the last decade there have been vast changes in the city's traditional reputation. From it being a typical 9 to 5 city, Islamabad has become more lively with many new restaurants and hotels springing up to service this new wealth. A lot of international food chains have opened, and generally a great improvement in nightlife with increasing shopping areas opening till late. However during winter season streets are considerably quiet after dark.

Even now, Islamabad remains a city where people enjoy its peaceful, calm atmosphere with a lot of greenery and nice surrounding scenery, very different from any other big city in Pakistan. It also serves as a base camp for people from the south and coastal areas like Karachi visiting valleys like Swat Valley Islamabad' Eastern end is dominated by mainly Federal Government offices, Parliament House, the official residences of the President and Prime Minister along with the Diplomatic Enclave, an area next to the Parliament House dedicated to foreign embassies. The population of the city has grown from 100,000 in 1951 to 1.15 million as of 2011.

You'll soon notice that Islamabad is laid out on a grid system with E7, F6, F7, G6, G7 being the oldest sectors, F8, F10, F11, G10, G11, I8 being where the 'new money' has been invested. E8, E9 are occupied by military housing complexes and are effectively out-of-bounds, G7, G8 and G9 are the heart of the city where many locals go for good bargain shopping, i.e. Karachi Company and Weekly Bazaars, and tasting the local cuisines, i.e. melody food park. The H and I sectors are a hotchpotch of mixed use residential, academic and industrial areas. E11, E12 and even now D12 are under construction, there is even a G13 being built up. F6 and F7 are where most of the action happens, but the number of embassies and powerful Pakistani's dwelling in these areas means a lot of securit and concrete barriers that are largely absent elsewhere. Choosing your guesthouse F6 & F7 may be your best bet.

Islamabad sits right next to Rawalpindi, the city that houses the Army headquarters. Also called the "twin cities", the difference in terms of atmosphere is striking: the green, calm and spacious Islamabad on the one side, the dense and noisy Rawalpindi on the other hand.

Climate
Islamabad features a very mild version of humid subtropical climate with abundant rainfall year-round. It features cool winters (mainly due to its altitude) and nighttime temperatures can drop below zero occasionally, but they usually stay between 1-3°C (33-37°F). Sparse snowfalls can occur in the surrounding hills but very rarely on the city itself. The lowest recorded temperature is -4°C (25°F). The area though does feature hot

summers with the average temperature being 31.2°C (88.2°F) in June, and in the afternoon 40°C (104°F) can be reached. The arrival of the monsoon does decrease temperatures a bit, but it brings intense amounts of rainfall (586mm or 22.7 inches, fall in July and August alone).

Get in
By plane
Islamabad International Airport (IATA: ISB) is a brand new terminal opened on 3rd May 2018 replacing the old Benazir Bhutto International Airport in Rawalpindi. Once notoriously bad, the new airport terminal is equipped with modern facilities for passengers. The new airport is situated in the west of Islamabad near Fateh Jhang and receives flights from a variety of international destinations, including in Europe via Turkish Airlines' hub in Istanbul (from

London, Manchester, Birmingham, Amsterdam, Geneva, Zurich, Frankfurt, Paris, and many more), the middle east through Dubai (via Emirates, Pakistan International Airlines PIA),Shaheen Air), Sharjah (AirBlue), Muscat, Doha, and Baghdad (Iraqi Airways)) and other Asian cities such as Urumqi (China Southern Airlines) and Bangkok (Thai Airways). Direct flights from London by British Airways resumed in June 2019. Also direct flights from London and Manchester to Islamabad by Virgin Atlantic has been started from December10, 2020.

Worth noting that other international destinations are served direct from Karachi and Lahore, including the only link to central Asia (Uzbekistan Airways fly from Lahore to Tashkent). A taxi from the airport to Islamabad is around Rs800 (in a yellow non a/c cab). You can easily walk out of the airport and hail a taxi to get a cheaper price. The white Toyota Corolla aircon radio cabs will set you back Rs800. Islamabad airport can get busy, meaning giving yourself 2-3 hours prior to departure is a good idea.

By bus
Niazi Express , Skyways Faisal_Movers and Daewoo Sammi are some of the nicer long-haul operators. Skyways offer some direct services to/from Islamabad and Lahore, Peshawar and Karachi. Daewoo has its own terminal on the road from Islamabad just outside Rawalpindi. The majority of buses arrive and depart from Rawalpindi, a few kilometers and a 45 minute taxi ride from Islamabad. Daewoo terminal can also be reached via Chamman Metrobus line, part of the Rawalpindi-Islamabad Metrobus

Corridor. It's best to book Daewoo by phone in advance if possible. At the moment they serve Karachi, Peshawar, Lahore, Murree, Sialkot, Abottabad, Bahawalpur, Faisalabad and Multan.

By train
The city is served by two major railway stations namely Islamabad Railway Station (also called Margala on Pakistan Railways Website) and Rawalpindi Railway Station, in the neighboring city of Rawalpindi. The First Class travel with Pakistan Railway is good and Rawalpindi has frequent railway connections with various major cities including Karachi, Lahore & Peshawar. The Islamabad Railway Station is located in Sector I-9 and can be reached by Khayaban-e-Johar Metrobus line whereas Rawalpindi Railway Station is located in Saddar and can be reached

via Saddar Metrobus Station which is 20 mins (1.5 km) by walk.

Get around
Metro Bus: goes through the center of the city from one end to the other, covering whole of Blue Area and most of the 9th Avenue. Metro Buses have good air conditioning systems and free wi-fi. Cost is fixed at Rs.20 for all distances. One can travel via combination of Metro and Taxis for getting into the sectors.

City Tour Bus: is new hop-on hop-off style bus service recently launched by Pakistan Tourism Development Corporation (PTDC). The bus take tourists to most of Islamabad's top attractions including Saidpur Village, Faisal Mosque, Pakistan Monument, Lok Virsa Museum and Lake View Park (Bird Aviary). The tour starts at 9 am from Flashman Hotel in Rawalpindi and ends at around 3 pm. PKR 500 for Students/ 600 for others and include the entry fees for all attractions.

Taxis: in Islamabad are abundant, popular and generally safe. Cost is around Rs70 Rs100 per sector traveled, depending on your bargaining skills. Prices will be higher at night, especially departing from places like Jinnah Super (F-7). It is always advisable to agree the fare before traveling. 'Uber', 'Sawaary' and the Dubai based 'Careem', are also both available at all times, at reasonable prices.

Car Hire: is also a good way of getting around. Although road signs and directions are only available on main roads, the city's grid and numbering system make it relatively easy to find your way around. There are various car hire companies in Blue Area F-6 and also in G-8 Markaz where cars can be hired with drivers. Most major hotels have their own car hire services and are relatively cheap. A tip to the driver at the end of the booking period is appreciated but not mandatory.

- ✓ Pak Car Rentals:, Office # 08, Street # 49, New Abpara Market, G-6/1, Islamabad, +923215467220. 24/7. Best Rent A Car service in town. Your car is just a call away from your doorstep. Providing doorstep delivery 24/7 with never ending reliable backup support call: +92 321 5467220 2500/=PKR.

See
Museums & Art Galleries
- ✓ Lok Virsa Museum, Shakarparian Park (next to H7 & G8) US$5 for foreigners. Recently

renovated, a delight. Definitely worth a visit. Islamabad's premier museum featuring more than 25 large galleries in four blocks linked through passages depicting cultural linkages with Iran, Central Asia and China. There are large halls dedicated to architecture, musical heritage, textiles, romances, Sufi shrines and several other cultural themes. It has a large collection of embroidered costumes, jewellery, woodwork, metalwork, block printing, ivory and bone work on display. The Heritage Reference Library of Museum has a great collection of data on art, music, history and crafts of all regions of Pakistan. Books on culture, heritage, audio and video cassettes of folk and classical vocal and instrumental music are sold at the Lok Virsa's Sales

Centre. Lok Virsa celebrates the national events in a befitting manner with musical concerts, exhibitions and public film shows on cultural heritage.

- ✓ Golra Pakistan Railways Heritage Museum, Golra Sharif train station (west of F11 (look on google maps)), 051 4316954. 8AM-4PM. A little known gem worth seeking out for a trip back in time to the glory days of the North West Railway the station house has been renovated and houses a small museum, and several old locomotives and rolling stock are there to be explored. Makes a nice cycle-ride from Islamabad. Rs 5.

- ✓ Pakistan Museum of Natural history this is more a place for school trips than a tourist destination however an impressive blue whale skeleton has recently been constructed outside

- ✓ National Art Gallery (F5/1) Opened in 2007, the gallery is a modern, light filled, air conditioned edifice that would not be out of place in many european cities. A diverting collection of almost 450 art pieces, purchased or gifted by the artists for National Art Gallery. Covers a surprising diversity of contemporary and classical paintings, sculpture and other installations. The Gallery is also home to an indoor and outdoor theatre (word-of-mouth and local press for schedules). Open 7 days a week from 11AM-1PM (free) and 2PM-7PM (Rs. 500) hence it is empty in the afternoons and you may find yourself trailed by gallery staff turning the lights on and off for you!

Located in F5/1, on the corner of Jinnah & Constitution avenues, opposite the Parliament building.

✓ Private art galleries are at the centre of Islamabad's art scene, with new exhibitions opening almost weekly. The three main gallaries are:

✓ Rohtas Gallery House 57-B, Street 26, F6/2, 051 2271390 , Nomad Gallery House 22, Justice Abdul Rashid Avenue, F6/1, 051 2273725 , and Kuch Khaas House 1, Street 2, F-6/3, 051-8357483. There is also the Jhoraka Art Gallery House # 8, Street 28 F8/1 .

Parks, viewpoints and green spaces

✓ Daman-e-Koh, a lookout point in the hills above E-6 with great views of the city on a clear day/night. Its beauty is enhanced by the greenery and flowers at different sites. High quality restaurants, good food, live music, hiking trails and lush green hillsides make it a favorite place for local and foreign tourist alike.

- ✓ Shakarparian a beautiful wild and hilly area for a nice evening walk in a green natural atmosphere. Is located south of G6 and G7.

- ✓ Japanese Park, is a children's park located near Islamabad Zoo. It is popular among children, families and to those visiting Islamabad from other cities due to its park facilities and children swing facilities.

- ✓ Rawal Lake has recently been upgraded by the Capital Development Authority. On the north side is Lake View Park (access from the road to Murree) a beautifully laid out park with gardens, picnic spots, and secluded paths and views over the lake. Is now home to an aviary, go-kart track and climbing wall. The terraced garden and the lake are used for fishing and boating. On the south side of the lake is another small park with a nice lookout, Red Onion restaurant and old Hindu temple. The highest point in the garden offers a panoramic view of Islamabad. Boating, sailing, water skating and diving facilities are organized by private clubs. To the west of the lake is the Islamabad Club, which offers different sporting facilities.

- ✓ Fatima Jinnah Park; also known as the F-9 park is considered one of the largest in South East Asia. F9 park is ideal for jogging around, and also has a cricket ground and some tennis court (minus nets). The park also has a large children's playground, some interesting sculptures, and an indoor facility with a nice bowling alley.

- ✓ Pir Sohawa. An overlook of Islamabad located in the Margalla Hills above the city. There are now two eateries at Pir Sohawa and both worth visiting. A walk up from Trail 3, from F-6/3 will get you to the hill top in around 2 hours with the perfect appetite, but you can reach Pir Sohawa by road in around 35-40 minutes.

- ✓ Rose & Jasmine Garden is located near Islamabad sports complex & Jinnah Stadium. South of Shahrah-e-Kashmir road and east of Islamabad Highway. Not too far from Rawal Lake.

- ✓ Ankara Park is a Turkish themed Garden adjacent to Rose & Jasmine Garden.
- ✓ Margalla Hills. Take a nice nature walk in the hills surrounding Islamabad, see trails below.

Mosques, shrines & monuments

- ✓ Faisal Masjid, Islamabad's most recognizable landmark, a very large mosque gifted by King Faisal of Saudi Arabia. Beautiful in the day or night, definitely worth the short taxi ride. Dress and act respectfully, this is much more a place of serious worship than a tourist site. Is open to non-Muslims outside of prayer times, but is sometimes shut altogether.
- ✓ National Monument near Shakarparian, represents Pakistan's four provinces and

three territories. From air the monument looks like a star (center) and a crescent moon (formed by walls forming the petals), these represent the star and crescent on Pakistan's flag. Also a small museum and a nice view of the city.

- ✓ Imam Bari Shrine Historical shrine of a Sufi saint located in the valley of NurPur Shahan near G5.

- ✓ Golra Sharif Shrine of Pir Mehr Ali Shah(rahmatullahi alayh), a Sufi Saint located in a village of Golra (Islamic religious site). Within the sanctuary of the shrine is the blessed grave of Hazrat Pir Meher Ali Shah Sahib Golravi rahmatullahi alayh, his son Hazrat Babu Jee Peer Sayyid Ghulam Muhyuddin Shah Sahib Golravi, his grandson Hazrat Baray Lala Jee Peer Sayyid Ghulam

Muinuddin Shah Sahib Golravi and his great-grandson, Hazrat Naseer e Millat Peer Sayyid Ghulam Naseeruddin Naseer Shah Sahib rahmatullahi alayh

Other

- ✓ Islamabad Zoo is located at the foot of Daman-e-Koh view point. It has more than 300 animals including 200 birds of different kinds, and tigers, lions and other animals, albeit in conditions that are not adequate for the wild animals.
- ✓ Blue Area, is Islamabad's financial and commercial center along the main arterial road Jinna Avenue which leads up to the main government buildings at the Constitution Avenue.

- ✓ Saidpur Village used to be a sleepy little village lying in the foothills of the Margallas with a mystic past and breathtaking natural beauty. It has now been remodeled. The village now become popular with the citizens of Islamabad who want an occasional break from the frenzy of urban life. Surrounded with lush, tranquil wilderness, the centuries old village is furnished with rustic fittings and offers amenities like a wide range of local food outlets and restaurants. Exhibitions are held regularly to show case the traditional arts, crafts and the rich cultural heritage of Pakistan.

- ✓ Attend open-air theater or just sit by the Lotus lake and relax. Check to see if there are is anything happening. The schedules are entirely calendar and weather dependent.

✓ Chattar bagh is a small park in the hills, around 25 minutes away from Islamabad. A water park with a few amusement rides, but will not offer much excitement for those who have seen other amusement parks or water parks.

Do
Rock Climbing There are many spots for rock climbing in Margalla Hills, Islamabad. Few crags have been developed but, still a lot of potential available to explore virgin lines. Jungle Rock (F 6a:8a), God Rock (F 6b+:7b), Legacy Wall (F 6a:7c+), Jasmin Corner (F 4b:5a), Belvedere (F 4c:6b+), Hidden Rock (F 6a:6c), Music Lounge (F 5c:6c) Beetle's Nest (F 5b:6c+, including multi-pitch route), Well Hidden Rock (F 5a:8a), Holiday

Rock (F 5b:5b), Said Pur View (F 5c:8a) and Shaddarrah (F 5c:6a) have been excellently developed/ bolted. There is also an artificial climbing wall in Rawal Lake's Lake View Park.

Horseback Riding
Ms Orrick is a Canadian qualified riding instructor who has lived and taught horseback riding for 6 years in Islamabad. She is well known for her patience, providing a fun-oriented approach as well as her kindness to horses. She can be reached at 0300 850 4220 or orrickw@hotmail.com.

Cycling – Cycling is becoming a popular activity and also a mode of transport because of the suitable weather, scenic beauty and peace of Islamabad. As active in more than 300 cities around the world, the group called Critical Mass is also present in Islamabad. The group sets out at a set location and time (co-ordinated through its facebook page), to pedal through set routes around and inside the city every Sunday. In addition, the Margalla Hills provide opportunities to do offroad Mountain Biking. MTB Islamabad is a mountain biking club and a knowledge base for offroad trails in the Margallas.

New and second hand bikes can both be purchased and rented in a few small shops in Islamabad and Rawalpindi as well. Good quality bikes are available from K2Riders based in F8/2 and Aerocycling, Shop 12; Block 12-D, G-8 Markaz.

Go karting F1 TraxxLake View Park (Rawal Lake) there is another track in Bahria Town, Rawalpindi

Shooting Islamabad Gun Club

Golf at the Islamabad Golf Club (next to the . Two other golf courses are available in Rawalpindi

Fishing – Rawal lake

Para Gliding – at Margalla Hills. The Pakistan Adventure Foundation is the place to call and reserve.

Rowing at the Islamabad Rowing Club, next to Lake View Park

Night Life – it exists, but it's not easy to find. Try befriending some hip locals, and see if you can tag along. There are no regularly open 'night clubs' in the city however periodic special events are organised in various venues about once every two months spread by word-of-mouth and increasing via Facebook. Less excitingly some of the embassy clubs in the diplomatic enclave have 'dance parties' and the like but these tend to be exclusively expatriate and rather low brow. See Jenny's List for details. Keep in mind that purchasing or consuming alcohol in Pakistan is illegal.

- ✓ Potohari Art & Craft Village (Starting soon), Shakarparian Near Rose and Jasmine Garden (Just across the Kashmir Highway on 7th Avenue). 11AM to 7PM. A craft bazaar with a food court serving 5 regional cuisines plus 3 Chai Khanas serving assorted teas and snacks. Built by the local Capital Development Authority but conceptualised and supervised by the Indus Heritage Trust.
- ✓ Asia Study Group, Above Dunkin Donuts, Blue Area, 051 2875891. Tu-Su 3-6PM. Running for nearly 40 years the ASG

organises various events, including seminars, hikes, weekend trips and the like principally for expats but also Pakistani's. Rs. 2,000 annual membership.

Walking in the Margalla Hills

The Margalla Hills are effectively foothills of the Himalayas and are starting directly at the North-Western edge of the city. There are a number of trails, some frequently used especially on weekends, others rarely. Keep in mind that the Margallas are quite big, steep hills, and shouldn't be underestimated, especially n the warmer months and during the heat of the day – if you are planning on a walk up to the top of the first ridge (ie where the Monal restaurant is) then sturdy footwear, a large water bottle, and a change of t-shirt are necessary (good chance you'll be drenched in sweat by the time you get to the top). Between March and November it is best to start walking in the early morning (start before 7-8AM) as it is uncomfortably hot during the day. Give the monkeys a wide berth, as they can be aggressive, especially if you display food.

There are many trails to choose from, some of which have been numbered by the city planners. The most popular walks are Trail 3 and Trail 5.

Trail 1 winds its way up to the ridge, where you can turn right and reach the Pir Sohawa road, near the turn-off for Talhaar. Takes about 2 hours to get to the top. From Pir Sohawa road its a 20 minute walk to the Monal restaurant, and you can catch a taxi back in to town, or head down Trail 3 or the Saidpur village trail.

Trail 2 / Zoo trail – Trail 2 begins a little way up Pir Sohawa road (just past the Jungle Shack drinks bar – GPS 33.7346°, 73.0545°) or you can start from the right of the entrance of the Islamabad Zoo. This is a good choice if you are looking for a 1-2 hour walk – the trail leads up to the Daman-e Koh viewpoint – if you want to continue walking a trail up to Cactus Ridge leads from next to the Police checkpoint near the entrance to Daman-e Koh. From Cactus Ridge you get a good view of where AirBlue flight 202 crashed.

Trail 3 begins from Margalla Road, F-6/3 (the junction between Margalla Road & Ataturk Avenue). It is a little steep and strenuous in the first leg, which goes up to the Viewpoint and is about a 30 50 min. trek. After the Viewpoint you can continue on for another easy-going 45 60 mins and reach the Pir Sohawa, where you can choose from 3 restaurants for food, The Monal,

Treehouse and Capital View Restaurant. This is the most popular walk, hence litter levels are high.

Trail 4 – This is the trail that goes into the hills from just 1km along the road after the Zoo. Due to the noise from the road that is on the other side of the valley, this trail is rarely used and somewhat overgrown. But it's worth a hike, especially if combined with Trail six.

Trail 5 also begins from Margalla Road in F-5 (about 500m down from Trail 3 opposite Judge's Enclave) and starts very gently in order to climb steeply later on. One option of Trail 5 connects with Trail 3 after Trail 3's viewpoint. If you continue on Trail 5 straight ahead instead, you eventually meet the Pir Sohawa road (33.7675°, 73.0771°). A third option is to veer east, ending up on the top of the ridge that leads down towards G5. Either way you'll eventually hit the Pir Sohawa road so it's difficult to get truly lost. From the top of Trail 5 it is 1.5km to the top of Trail 3 – hence you can do a loop, taking 3 – 4 hours.

Trail 6 – also known at the E7 or Faisal Mosque trail. Head to the carpark to the rear of the Faisal Mosque, and look for the Margalla Hills visitor center. Head through the gate, after a few meters leave the main track that turns to the left and continue straight on the smaller trail. Follow the valley bottom and river until the trail leaves the river bed and climbs to the right. This is the direct and quite steep option. The longer, more shaded and less steep option continues along the river bed before climbing towards the right. After passing a spring and then an abandonned farm, it meets the first, direct trail option. Then continue to a saddle which connects to the valley in which the Pir Sohawa road is going up. Here you can take trail 4 on the right to go down towards the road. Or go left to reach the main ridge.

There is another trail further east, sometimes also called Trail 6 in the valley to the east of Trail 5. Start from the Trail 5 carpark, walk parallel to the blocked off dual carriageway heading east and then head north when you see the mouth of the valley. Walk past a small cluster of houses and then you'll come across a sealed single track road, follow this for a short while and you'll end up on the path, and follow this up the valley, ascending to the left side. You'll eventually end up on the Pir Sohawa road. From here you can head west to the top of Trail 5. The Trail is without signposts or markers, is little used but very scenic.

Saidpur trail follow the river through the village (including ducking though some back alleys) and you'll emerge in a valley and a trail that leads up to the Monal restaurant and hence you can easily do a loop coming down Trail 3. Saidpur trail isn't much used .

Bari Imam trail – for the more adventurous this is a good hike. Drive to Nurpur Shahan (east of the government complexs beyond the end of Margalla Road) – head to a road junction at 33.7457°, 73.1050° and turn left, until you reach a turnoff for a small guesthouse at the start of the trail (33.7569°, 73.1135°). The walk starts with steps leading up to the Bari Imam cave, then you can continue up the steep hill behind, then traverse round to the Pir Sohawa road, where there are a few cafes and a hotel (33.7843° , 73.1107° – it is about 5km from here to the Top of Trail 3 if you follow the road). You can return down the valley back to your starting point. Beware however that you pass into Khyber Paktunkwa on the walk and you may have to charm yourself pass some policemen.

Both Trail 3 & Trail 5 & Trail 6 have large maps and guidance boards placed at the entrance. Marking on the trails is limited, but on most trails, there are many people on the weekends. So it's difficult to get lost.

For more walks and information buy a copy of Hiking Around Islamabad (available in Saeed Book Bank in F7 Markaz) or read through the original 1992 version. Also read this blog about some of the best hiking trails in the Margalla Hills.

Buy

Islamabad is divided into sectors, each sector having its own central shopping area (or markaz) where all local amenities are located. Some of the more popular markazes are the F6 Markaz (aka Supermarket) F7 Markaz (aka Jinnah Market), G6 Markaz (aka Melody Park), G9 Markaz (aka Karachi Company) and so on. There isn't much going on in the markets of F8, G7 an G8 that would interest the tourist. Each markaz has its own peculiarities and each one is worth visiting individually. However most things are catered for in each markaz i.e. clothing, shoes, fast food etc. There's always a real buzz in the evenings when all the shoppers come out, particularly in the run up to Eid.

- ✓ 7th Avenue, located at Jinnah Super Market (F7 Markaz), has large selection of western food products.

Metro, located way out in I11 is a huge Walmart type store selling groceries and household goods. Prices are good but not the cheapest in Islamabad but if you are looking for a western style shopping trolley experience this is your best bet.

- ✓ Handicrafts, The Capital Development Authority, has recently established a handicrafts village near super market, where small stalls with handicrafts from around the country are available. You should be able to walk from there to Mahraja (next to united Bakery) and find plenty of other stores much larger and with a much better collection of handicrafts and traditional items. This is a MUST visit for all first time visitors and a useful stop for quick gift items for people back home. A good present for the ladies is Pashmina shawls or wraps, which can cost anywhere between $15 to as much as $700. Remember to bargain, you will be charged Gora price.

- ✓ Art See above. Some of the places to visit are, Khaas, The National Art Gallery and Nomad Art Gallery.

- ✓ Music Peak Shop 4, Amant Plaza, Main Double Road, F10 markaz. Small modern music shop, with guitars and other instruments.

- ✓ Haroons, the perfect place to shop for gifts and women accessories. Is in Super Market.

- ✓ Saeed Book Bank is the largest bookstore in the city, located in the F-7 Markaz. A wide variety, from old books of local interest ("The Story of the Malakand Field Force" by Churchill, for instance) to modern best-sellers, as well as greeting cards. Plenty about geopolitics and war in Pakistan and Afghanistan as well. A must-visit destination.

- Furniture: There a are a number of places selling antique or new furniture made from antique wood pieces, such as Wood Heritage, and another small but packed one in E-7.
- Octave Guitar Shop & Music Lessons (Musical Instrument Store), Shop No. 5, Basement of Pehchan Mall, Mall 9, G-9 Markaz, Islamabad, 03335342184.

Shopping malls in capital

- ✓ The Centaurus, Everything in one package from multiplex to food court. Also has a "Fun City" for children. Clean, well-organized, and ou can get all multinational companies there under one roof, though it's light on local flavor, though there are many local clothing stores. It is the most popular and largest mall in the city.

- ✓ World Trade Center, Also known as Giga Mall, WTC is a huge shopping mall with several branded stores including handicraft stores. The mall is amongst 326 WTC's operating in about 100 countries with 750,000 affiliations. It was opened in 2016 with three levels of shopping, eating and entertainment including a Fun City for children, cinema and a hypermarket.

- ✓ Safa Gold Mall, At F-7 Markaz. Has slighter cheaper options available at the food court, but otherwise the shop selection is inferior to that of Centaurus. It also hosts a lot of events, and is also usually not very crowded. Has a 4-D cinema.
- ✓ Mall9, At G-9 Markaz.
- ✓ Al Taqwa Mall, Good shopping mall with food court and playland.

Foreign Currency Exchange is easily available from F-6 Blue Area where there are 100s of money changers in privately owned shops. It is advised to check the rate with a few of them before going ahead with it.

Eat
At first glance the visitor may feel that Islamabad offers little to excite the taste-buds, however beneath the surface there is a thriving restaurant

scene. Many of the better restaurants are away from the main markets of F6 and F7. Most do not serve alcohol, but some allow you to bring your own. Call ahead to ask.

Food poisoning is a significant concern when eating out in Islamabad. Food safety and proper storage are in their nascent stages in Pakistan, and stomach issues plague most visitors at some point. Avoiding raw fruits and vegetables is prudent.

For ease of use restaurants are organised by sector:

F6

- ✓ Majlis, Hill Road (northern end, on the F6-3 side), a trendy place with good Lebanese food. A place where you will find the the movers and shakers of the city and a large portion of the Arabic diplomatic community. The food is pretty good (although some would argue that the Lebanese Cafe in F10 is more authentic), and the setting just right. Though those visiting on a tight budget can choose to avoid it, it sure is worth a stop. It also delivers.

- ✓ Mango Tree / Nana's Kitchen, 2 Hill Road F6/3 (old UN Club building), 051 2279313. lunch & dinner. Tastefully understated refurbishment of the old UN club building. Mango Tree offers great Thai food, a delicate combination of fresh ingredients and authentic Thai flavours. A bit pricey the owners play the old trick of slapping on 17% tax and 10% service to the bill, hence mains are about Rs 700 a pop. The upstairs balcony is particularly pleasant. Downstairs Nana's kitchen serves up a decent lunch and dinner menu with Brunch on Sundays. And their cupcakes are famous in Islamabad. The decor is tastefully done in soft tones and is accented by a large beautifully built fireplace.

- ✓ Table Talk, Khosar Market, 051 227-1927. lunch and dinner. understated, home-cooked, well presented Asian and European food, in a small, cosy inside-outside restaurant with London Books (shop) next door. The place is aimed squarely at the expat market, and priced with this in mind. Owner also runs Riffy's restaurant in Chak Sharzad call for details.

- ✓ Khiva offers a Central Asia Cuisine. It has indoor and outdoor seating. Address: House no.64, Main Margalla Road, F-6/3, Islamabad

- ✓ Nandos, F6 super market, south side. lunch and dinner. recently opened branch of the popular chicken chain mains Rs 300.

- ✓ Cafe Khaas, No. 1, Street 2, F-6/3. Cafe Khaas, is an extension of Khaas Art Gallery. A lunch only place that is normally packed, though expensive has great food. They also boast one of the finest art collections in Islamabad. Look for "Mouse" or the manager, and you will be given personal attention. Make sure you get a suggestion for what is best, and work your way through the limited, but exquisite menu. At the lunch hour, this place is filled with yet more, movers and shakers of Islamabad, from the business men, to politicians, models and expats. The place is always kicking for the sophisticated lunch.

- ✓ Luna Caprese, 34 School Road, F-6/3 (look for a house with L C on the gates), +92-51-2825061. Famous for being the site of a bomb attack in 2008, offers acceptable Italian dining with an extensive menu covering, pastas, seafood and meat. Wine and beer available at a price (Rs 600 for a glass of red). Nice garden out back. pricey.

- ✓ Cafe Melange House 6, Street 41, F-6/1. Eat in, take away or delivery. Pizza is some of the best in Islamabad. 023 136 352 643

F7

- ✓ Espresso Lounge, F-7 Markaz (Jinnah Super), Behind Shell Petrol pump and standard Chartered Bank. Best Cafe of the town.

Specialize in a variety of coffees, pastas, salads, sandwiches, desserts. 051-2652943

- ✓ Upper Deck, F-7 Markaz (Jinnah Super), above Gourmet Bakery, near north-west corner of Markaz. A very nice, up-market restaurant specializing in seafood. Popular with expats and well-off locals. Nice ambiance, a variety of well-prepared fish, fish & chips and a fish burger. Decent cheesecake and chocolate cake for dessert. Main courses Rs300 Rs800.

- ✓ Namak Mandi, 51 Bhittai Road, F7/1 (Opposite to Telenor Head Office). Only for dinner. Set in a pleasant garden behind a large guest house. Pakistani food, traditional music playing, aimed firmly at expats. Service is slow but the food good. Drinks available at a price (Rs2,500 for a bottle of wine). There is a better restaurant with the same name in Rawalpindi

- ✓ Signature, 47a Bhittai Road (opp. F7 markaz), 051 2651804-5. lunch & dinner. Opened in May 2011 and after a patchy start this place has found its feet. Tastefully decorated house restaurant offering an excellent choice in European dishes try the Mediterranean chicken with olives, prunes & sun-dried tomatoes or the chocolate hazelnut timbale for dessert. The resident pianist adds to the occasion. Together with the Polo Lounge this is one of Islamabad's best restaurants. Can bring your own drinks. Recommended. mains from Rs600.

- ✓ Papa Sallis, F-7 Markaz (Jinnah Super)(Ph: 2650550-3), Very well known place (Please ask any local shop for directions) for steaks and pizzas since 1991. Prices are quite high for Pakistani standards, but from a Western perspective still very cheap.

- ✓ Kitchen Cuisine / KC Grill, 81 Bhittai Road, F7/4 (just off the southeast corner of Jinnah Super) 051 2655712. Adequate cafe restaurant with a nice terrace serves european and Pakistani cuisine at reasonable prices (mains Rs 400). There is a popular bakery with really fresh and tasty bakery products downstairs, including chocolate fudge cakes, cheese cakes and low cholesterol items. Made to Order services are also available.

- ✓ Ye Olde Hangout, F-7 Markaz (Jinnah Super), behind Shell petrol station. A wonderful little coffee shop/sheesha bar. They serve a small selection of global and local food, and play sexy Bollywood and Egyptian videos. Posters of Jimi Hendrix, 50 Cent, Marilyn Manson and Angus Young are on the walls. One room is all men. Another for mixed couples and ladies only. No alcohol of course, but lots of cigarettes and a good tea selection.

- ✓ Civil Junction, F-7/3 markaz (Gol Market) offers good coffee and an interesting array of drinks and 'mocktails'. Light snacks are also offered along with coffee and drinks. The place offers occasional live music from upcoming local bands, making it a popular hangout with the youth of the city.

- ✓ Hot Spot, One of the few places that Islamabad can claim as theirs first. F-7/3 (Gol Market) also offers a great ice-cream place. Though the menu has now increased from just ice-cream to milkshakes, pies, sandwiches and plenty more, the place still has the feel of an ice-cream joint. With a unique, rather artistic decor, Hot Spot is a must visit for any first time traveler to Islamabad.

- ✓ Pizza Hut, F7 Markaz (near Saeed Book Bank), 051 111 241 241. Not the same as worldwide, but still better than a few.

- ✓ Clique Cafe, House 10-A, Street 13, Sector F-7/2, 051-2608965. 12 noon 11PM. Opened in 2010 this place is still trying to establish itself. Its Euro-russian menu and tasteful modern décor make it worth seeking out. Mains Rs. 500.

- ✓ Olive Garden, Street No.4, Goll Market, F7/3, 051-2610914. lunch until late. Set in the wealthy back streets of F7 the Olive

Garden is popular with wealthy Pakistani's and is a great place to people watch on a weekend. Food is variable, but the setting is nice, with a fire pit in winter, and plenty of sheesha. Not part of the American chain. Rs. 500 for mains.

- ✓ Kabul Restaurant, F-7 Markaz (Jinnah Super), +91 51 265 0953. 11AM-10PM. This large restaurant just off the markaz serves up tasty kebabs and Afghani specialties, and is usually very crowded with locals and expats at dinner time. Mains Rs 75-200.

- ✓ Seoul Club Korean Restaurant, House 21a, Street 55, F7/4, 03015063354. 7-11PM. Hidden away in F7's back streets is this house-converted-to-restaurant run by a Korean women. Most other diners are Korean expats craving a taste of home.

Most Korean favourites available, including dolsot bibimbap, and piles of Kimchi. No 'cook at your table' bulgolgi however. Moderately expensive. Alcohol available, but ask the price before ordering.

- ✓ Street 1 Cafe, Khosar Market, F/6-3. 06-23PM. Securely placed in Kohsar Market which is frequented by westerner living as diplomats/families in Islamabad. 300-1000.

- ✓ MJ's Coffeehouse and Bakery. After 4 successful years in F10, now in Jinnah Super, Bhitai Road. 051 2608112 and 2608113. 8AM-11 PM. Specialist European style bakery, pizzeria and coffeehouse. Excellent food, speciality breads, cheesecakes, gelato ices, Fondant designer cakes for those special moments.

F8

- ✓ China Town Restaurant, Street 55, F-8/4. A large and popular Chinese restaurant. It offers Sichuan Cuisine with Firepot as one of it's specialities coupled with the modern blend where the waiters use PDAs to take orders. China Town enjoys a very loyal patronage from its customers. The restaurant is being re-located to a beautiful 8,000 sq ft building on Street 55, F-8/4. It features a professional kitchen in the basement, a beautiful lounge on ground floor, a fine dining hall on the first floor, and a roof top sitting with a fantastic view of Margallas.

- ✓ Dumpling Zhang Chinese Restaurant, 32a Street 55 F8/4 (opp. the Christian church (there is no sign outside, just a security guard)), 051 2853623. 7-10PM. Low key

Chinese restaurant set in a suburban house, run by a Chinese family. Food is more authentically Chinese in comparison to the Pak-China food you get elsewhere in Islamabad, demonstrated by the fact that half your fellow diners will be from China. The potions are designed to share between 2 so remember to order half sizes. An added plus is that this place will serve you a cold beer with your food (Rs300 a bottle). Mains Rs300-700. Dumplings are especially good value at Rs300 for 30..

✓ Patio Lounge, House no. 1, street 17, F-8/3. Opened in May 2011 this place is still finding its feet. Tastefully furnished garden with wall mounted fans keeping down the summer heat. Menu is standard western fare, although the steaks are considerably better than average. Also serves Sheesha as a digestive.

- ✓ The House of Bombay, 18 Margalla Road, F8/3. 051 831 2705/6. Opened July 2011 this place is establishing itself as the place to go for decent south Asian cuisine. What separates HoB from the rest is that everything is made fresh and has a real home cooked taste to it and the cooking oil is kept to a minimum. Mains Rs700. Can bring your own drinks.

- ✓ Tahzeeb, 35 Park Road, F8/1, 051 2856513. lunch & dinner, closed Mondays. Recently opened high-end restaurant serving European and Pakistani cuisine. Good food (try the caramelised steak) good service, a pleasant garden and local art on the walls makes this place worth seeking out. Has a clothing boutique upstairs also. Mains Rs500-800.

- ✓ LA balto Sheesha bar it has a very good offering flavours as well as snacks pizzas too.. a great place to visit

- ✓ 19th House 6-A, Street 69, F8/3. 0345-5236578 / 051-8356280/1. Another Chinese restaurant set in a house, this one with a Shezhuan flavour. The chef, Ami Qin speaks both English and French.

- ✓ Urban Lounge Street 21, F8/2. A new coffee house opened up in 2011, this joint caters mostly to youngsters with its fairly budgeted and western food. The desserts are definitely worth a try and with ample seating at indoor sheesha allowed, its more than 90% of the time occupied!

- ✓ Habibi Restaurant Markaz F-8 (in the parking behind Habib Bank Ltd.) Serves Bar B Que and local dishes. During lunchtime mostly frequented by the crowd visiting "Kutchery" i.e. the Courts which are located in F-8 markaz.

F9

- ✓ McDonald's is situated in the south-west corner of the F-9 Park. It also has a drive through service. Very popular with families. Beware of crowds, as it is always full. Consider doing a take away on weekends.

F10

- ✓ Italian Oven, F10 Markaz, facing the Park, 051 2103133. Pleasant, locally orientated Italian restaurant extensive menu covering pizzas, pasta, meat and seafood and all done pretty well (except the pizzas). Nice views of the F9 park from the upstairs seating area. mains Rs 400.

- ✓ Lebanese Cafe, Tariq market f10/2 (just off street 14). Run by a Lebanese family, the cafe restaurant is the perfect excuse to delve in to the back streets of F10 the setting is nothing fancy, but the food is excellent, and very good value. Home deliveries available. No sheesha however.

- ✓ Eclipse Cafe, 3a Street 65, F10/3 (right at the end of Street 65), 0300 5277638. Young hip hangout in the back streets of F10 menu is simple but tasty, with many European favourites. Excellent rooftop sheesha bar. This is a popular place for Islamabad's young and wealthy. Open until late. mains Rs 350.

- ✓ Rock Bistro, Street 11a F10/2 (off Street 8), 051 2547764. Open until late. Worth visiting just to see the custom made building. Nestled in the suburban sprawl of F10 this place offers a varied menu covering many cuisines, and doing a pretty good job at most of them. One of the more memorable places to eat in the city and certainly worth seeking out. Mains Rs 450+.

- ✓ MJ's Specialities, MJ Plaza, Street 14, Tariq Market, F10/2 (from F10 Markaz take double road towards F11, last traffic lights turn right, then first right to street 14 and you are there), 051 2210371. 8AM-midnight. Specialist European style bakery, pizzeria and BBQ. Excellent food, specialty breads, cheesecakes, gelato ices. Outside lawn for BBQ.

- ✓ MJ's Coffeehouse, Street 14, Tariq Market, F10/2 (above MJ's Specialties), 051 2210371. 8AM-midnight. A little gem of a coffeehouse serving the best coffee this side of Gloria Jeans in F6. Serves proper coffee in tasteful surrounds, and a great collection of cakes to boot just a shame its all the way out in F10 Espresso Rs90.

"Inkantray" (Incantare) a nice place for hangout with friends. Mostly for shisha. In basement of Pizza Hut.

- ✓ Cafe Paprika, Butt Plaza, F-10 Markaz. Next to Standard Chartered Bank and Jamil Sweets., 051-2110606 or 051 2110607. A nice little cafe with an interesting and wide range of food menu. A definite choice to eat from for a scrumptious lunch or dinner. It is comparatively new as of 2013. generally between 250-1000.

F11

✓ Tapas Restaurant F11, Shop 8-9, Lords Trade Center, F11 Markaz, 051 2211911. 11AM-midnight. Restaurant, cafe, Spanish, Roll Parathas, Shawarma, Pastas, Chinese, Italian, Desi, BBQ. Home Delivery Dine Inn and Take Away mains Rs.400Rs.700.

E11

✓ Des Pardes A sister restaurant of the popular Pakistani eatery in Saidpur village. Someone has clearly spent some money on opening this place set in a huge tent in E11 markaz. Excellent Pakistani food, but you may find it quiet on a weeknight.

- ✓ Blak Lounge, E11/3 Markaz, 051-2228463. Overly stylish sheesha lounge and cafe, very much the modern face of Pakistan and a place to go to meet the hip, young and rich.

- ✓ Homestyle Cafe / Funky Bake swish cafe in E11 markaz, has a great little made-to-order cupcake setup (Funky Bake) attached.

G6

- ✓ Melody Food Park In Melody G-6 Markaz is a newly opened food area with variety of food to choose from with some nationally famous restaurant names having outlets there. Plenty of BBQ and traditional Pakistani food with a variety of fresh fruit juices to choose from.

- ✓ Rakaposhi, pastry shop at the Serena, has some of the best coffee and pastries in

Pakistan. Worth a visit if you just want to relax or get some work done. The Serena also offers wireless internet, so, it is an ideal place to sit and get some work done if you like.

- ✓ Kamran Restaurant In Aabpara, G-6/1 is also a famous place for traditional Pakistani cuisine.

- ✓ Real French Bakehouse At back side of Melody food park shop 9 block 21 is one of the leading baker of Islamabad producing a variety of French and local products with its expert team in a hygienic way. Cell 051-2603390.

- ✓ Nirvana Cafe and Spa, popular spot with 'ladies who lunch', business meet and greets and devotees of the tuna sandwich. House

18, Street 90, G-6/4. The thai red curry is good.

G9

- ✓ Khyber Afghan Restaurant, Street 55, G9/4. Pleasant local Afghan restaurant set in a small house, and a good excuse to explore the back streets of little-visited G9. Can eat well for under Rs. 500 per person.

- ✓ Tapas, Shop No. 1-3, St # 5, Mangla Road, Jehangir Market G-9/2, 051-2854455. 11AM-12AM (Midnight). The Only Spanish Restaurant in Islamabad with wide range of variety in food. Pastas, burgers, french fries, shawarmas, roll paratha, salads, Italian and soups.

I-8 Markaz

- ✓ Masoom's cafe, Anique Arcade, I-8 Markaz, 051-3029922. Small & pleasant cafe and pâtisserie, a place for lunch or a coffee rather than a dinner

- ✓ Habibi, Executive Center, I-8 Markaz, 051-4448222. Open until late. Upscale Afghan style BBQ restaurant with indoor and outdoor seating look for the big red sign

- ✓ Hot Plate, Shop 8, City Arcade, I8 markaz, 051 4862331. lunch & dinner. Notionally Italian in pleasant dark wood surroundings. Certainly I8's nicest looking restaurant. Serves a range of salads, pastas, steaks and sea food. Worth making the trip to I-8 for. Mains Rs400-500.

- ✓ Rayyan's, I-8 Markaz, +92-51-2855496. Fast Food Take Away,

- ✓ Haleem Ghar, I-8/1 Mughal Market, 051 4432606. Pakistani Cuisine Low Range.

Rahat Bakery is situated at I-8 Markaz having plenty of delicious items to eat.

Blue Area

- ✓ Red Onion Chain of Restaurants Blue Area, opposite the Saudi Pak Tower building stands one of the oldest restaurants in Islamabad. Established in 1991 with buy one, get one free pizza. Wide range of cuisines i.e Mexican, Italian, Chinese, Pakistani & Continental. Prices are moderate, ambiance is modern & service is friendly

- ✓ Lasania Restaurant, 66 West Junaid Plaza, Blue Area (Ph: 227-3200, 287-2200). This place is very nicely decorated and is also situated in a very nice location. They have a huge selection of BBQ, Pakistani and Chinese food items on the menu. Their food is not extremely spicy like most other places.

- ✓ The Terrace , 3rd Fl, Centaurus Mall is an outdoor food court of 5 restaurants and cafes including Daawat, Bhaati Gate, Wok Fusion Cafe, Gloria Jeans Coffee House and La Terrazza.

- ✓ Cinnamon, Beverley Center, Blue Area, 051 2206988. One of Islamabad's best European restaurants, serving a range of continental pastas, salads and meat dishes, as well as a range of refreshing mocktails. The décor is absolutely superb, with black and white motifs and photographs, and the service and quality of food equally good. The perfect place to have a quiet albeit slightly expensive dinner.

- ✓ The Cave, Awan Arcade, Blue Area (near the eastern end of Jinnah Avenue, north (F6) side), 051-2270595. lunch & dinner. Curious restaurant in a basement with a plasticy cave theme going on. Food is acceptable, with large portions of European (steakhouse) and Pakistani food. More curious than the restaurant itself is the fact that this place tops the listings for Islamabad. Mains around Rs400-500.

- ✓ Tehzeeb (formerly known as Rahat Bakers), F-6 Blue Area, Driving along the main road in blue area, with pizzas, bakery products, rich creamy milk ice creams etc are available. A big range to choose from. Although it is a fairly big store, there are no eat-in arrangements. Right next to Rahat Bakers is a place called Safilo, which offers a wide range of ice-creams, milkshakes and juices. They pride themselves in their cleanliness.

- ✓ Subway is a franchise of the international Subway and has two branches, one in Blue Area, and the other one in F11-Markaz. It offers subs and salad.

- ✓ Domino's Pizza, Block H, Blue Area, 051 111 366 466. Take away, dine in and free home delivery.

- ✓ Usmania Restaurant In Blue Area is also a famous place for traditional Pakistani cuisine.

- ✓ Bolan Saltish Afghani and Pakistani restaurant, known for its Khadda Sajji.

- ✓ Jahangir's, Masco Plaza, Blue Area is one of the most popular local restaurant chains. Its delicious local or 'desi' items and barbecue are a treat, garnering it lots of appreciation from food lovers. Known for their Pakistani and Indian specialties.

- ✓ Bar-B-Q Tonight (Bar-B-Q Tonight), Shorab Palaza, Block 32, FazlL-e-haq Road Islamabad. (on the G6 side of the Blue area, off A.K.M Fazl ul Haq road), 051-8317131, 051-8317132. 12-24. Popular new BBQ restaurant, with consistently good food and a varied menu of Pakistani favorites. Same owners as the branch in Karachi. Big rush on dinner timings. Price ranges from 300-700 per person. Free delivery available. 300+.

Diplomatic Enclave

- ✓ Kanpai, Street 4, Diplomatic enclave (near Standard Chartered Bank). Expensive but not bad Japanese restaurant, and one of the few restaurants in the Diplomatic enclave outside of an Embassy and hence open-to-all. Serves a range of Bento boxes, tempura, noodles, sushi and sashimi, and in all fairness the food is fairly authentic (the owner/manager is Japanese). Can bring your own drinks also. set meals from Rs. 1,000.

- ✓ Cordon Rouge, Embassy Road, Diplomatic Enclave. Lunch & dinner. Something of a diplomatic enclave institution. Cordon Rouge serves up authentic French cuisine in softly lit surroundings. A bit pricey but decent food. Extensive wine list.

Saidpur Village / Margalla hills

- ✓ Des Pardes, (In Saidpur village off the Margella Road), +92-51-2825151. lunch & dinner. A great choice for top notch Pakistani food evenings are best when Saidpur is illuminated with subtle floodlighting, and you can relax on the terrace and admire the architecture. Can be very busy on weekends so reserving a table is recommended the parking can be chaotic also. Mains Rs.400.

- ✓ Polo Lounge, Saidpur village, 051 282-1677. Decent fine dining restaurant, with a long established sister restaurant in Lahore. European menu, excellent steaks, professional chef, drinks available. The upstairs terrace is wonderful, if a bit chilly in winter. Reservations recommended. mains Rs.700+.

- ✓ Monal, Pir Sohawa (Road to Pir Sohawa starts from 7th Avenue at junction of F6 and F7), +92-51-7165915. Set at an altitude of 3900 ft on Margalla Hills, Monal offers a spectacular view of the city. It is the largest restaurant in Pakistan in terms of seating capacity

- ✓ Chicken Shack in Pir Sohawa about 5km past Monal a simple BBQ place with great views to the north and south. Mains about Rs300.

Rawal Lake

- ✓ Kinara, Jinnah Road, Bani Gala (On the southern bank of Rawal Lake. From Rawal Chowk take Park Road, after 2km turn left following signs for Bani Gala, follow this road for about 1km.). A lovely setting on the southern banks of Rawal Lake, and offering great sunset views over the water. Its all outdoor and set in a garden, with a few gazebos to shade you from the sun. Food is BBQ & standard Pakistani, and good value also. You may want to bring a map if its your first visit as its a little tricky to find.

- ✓ Red Onion Near the dam on the southern end of the lake. Standard food but a nice setting on the lakeside, with views across the water to Islamabad.

- ✓ Lake View Park Restaurant is the only place to eat on the northern part of the lake. Which is a shame as the place is over 1km from the waters edge and the food is overpriced for what you get.

Drink
Drinking alcohol in public is nominally banned although most of the top end hotels have their

own bars. The windowless basement sports bar in the Marriot is probably the most frequented of the hotel bars.

Most Pakistanis though would find it extremely rude and offensive if you show or drink alcohol in public.

Non-Muslim visitors can obtain from the local police a so called 'non-Muslim declaration'. This permit gives you the right to legally buy a limited amount of alcoholic drinks like bottles of wine or beer. For instance, Pakistan's small Christian minority is by law allowed to consume alcohol.

Try local brands like Murree Brewery, in addition to that there are other brands such as Budweiser and Bavaria with non-alchoholic beer. There is a small off-license around the side of the Marriot hotel (next to the dry cleaners) you'll need a 'non-Muslim declaration' (or maybe just a foreign passport if you turn on the charm) to be able to buy anything.

In soft drinks, all the usual western brands are available but better to try local limca cola which makes "pop" sound when opened. you can also try Pakola; Pakistan's premier soft drink brand which is available in different flavors like Ice cream soda, Lychee, Orange, Raspberry, Apple sidra, Vino, Double cola, Bubble up etc. A 'fresh lime 7-up' is a better alternative for people who don't like standard soft drinks.

In other drinks try strawberry milk shakes and dhamaka soda (dhamaka means bang the bang that happens when one opens the bottle) from Jinnah super market.

- ✓ Gelato Affairs (Gelato Affairs), F-6 (Main Kohsar Market), 0512610919.

- ✓ Mocca Coffee, Shop #1, Kohsar Market, F-6/3 (Main Kohsar Market). The classic expat coffee shop typically expensive with exclusive decor, display and sale of World-renowned contemporary Nordic design, such as Georg Jensen, Arne Jacobsen, Stelton, Eva-trio and Rosendahl.

- ✓ Jia's Deli, Beverly Centre, 0512814110. This café has a certain cosy charm. The low ceiling has photographs of their regular customers on display, and a few bright abstract oil paintings to brighten up its plain wooden walls. Bread is home made, and came in four varieties. Coffee is of extremely good quality, served with chocolates that appear to be hand-made:

salted caramel, walnut and tiramisu, mocha java cake flavours all works real well. The service is spot on, with even minor details such as the topping up of bread faultless. There is an array of desserts and some great cakes.

Sleep
Budget
Budget accommodation in Islamabad is fairly lackluster and questionably clean. There are many guesthouses around the city that make a nice alternative to a hotel.

- ✓ The Boys Hostel (TBH), G-8 (campus), F-10 (Campus) & G-10 (Campus). Phone: 2102352, 2256705, 2224012
- ✓ Hotel Blue Sky, Sitara Market, G-7 Markaz. Double rooms from Rs300, with cable tv from Rs. 400. Update: as of 03/2015 prices

are at least 1200 Rs for a room. Management is not friendly to women travelling alone and has limited English skills.

- ✓ Simara Hotel, Sitara Market, G-7 Markaz. With good bargaining skills you can get a double room for 1000 Rs (03/2015). Can be strange travelling alone as a woman. Also, only pay to the official receptionist and ask for a receipt.

- ✓ Hotel Friends Inn, Aabpara Market, G-6 Markaz. As of 09/2014, rates for single rooms were around 2300 Rs with A/C.

- ✓ Hotel Meraj Next to National Bank of Pakistan, G-9 Markaz, Karachi Company. Tel: +92 (0)51 2282587, 2255056-7 Double rooms from Rs. 1600

- ✓ Caravan Park Opposite Aabpara Market and a little distance away from the Shakarparian Hills. This place is open and accessible only for foreigners, making it exclusive and safe. Adequate facilities are provided to make visitors to the area comfortable and at home. Rs50 per person, Rs100 per vehicle (bicycles free). Popular with overlanders. Update: since the Nanga Parbat Attack in 2013, this place is closed.

- ✓ Sohawa Heights Hotel, Pir Sohawa Up in the Margalla Hills about 5km past the Monal restaurant. An alternative to staying in Islamabad proper is to stay up in the hills overlooking the city. Rooms are en suite, have satellite TV, and great views over the city (from the roof terrace) and view to the north over the picturesque valley behind from your bedroom. Only really an option if you have your own transport, as its a 30 minute drive from town up the hill. There is a popular restaurant (The Khokha) and some shops / restaurants nearby. Rs. 1,200 per room.

Mid-range

- ✓ Carnations Suites, House # 1A, Marvi Road F7/4, Islamabad. Phone: 0092 52 261 1450-51. Cell: 0092 333 53 222 14. Email: info@carnations_suites.com. Uniquely designed, intimate, cosy environment. Great place to stay. In the heart of the capital city; from here most of the sites are within short distance. Very enthusiastic and helpful staff, clean and nicely decorated rooms, bathrooms and kitchen. Good breakfast and free internet. .

- ✓ Cape Grace(New) Guest House, H 8, Justice Abdul Rasheed Road, F-6/1, +92 (300) 5252232 (newcapegrace@gmail.com). 3-star range GuestHouse with 5MB WiFi@Fiberoptic, air conditioning & heating, powerbackup. Starting from 2,500PKR per night.

- ✓ Chez Soi, 6 Kohsar Rd, F-7/3 (Nearby to Jinnah Super Market), +92 (51) 265-1451. Same owner as Upper Deck restaurant. Chez Soi has been hosting the diplomatic community exclusively since 1993. Starting around Rs4000/night..

- ✓ Continental House, 94-A Nazimuddin Road, F-8/4 (Near Centaurus), +92 (51) 2256670). starting around Rs 3,000/night.

- ✓ Continental Inn, 94-B Nazimuddin Road, F-8/4 (Opposite Centaurus and Blue Area),

+92 (51) 2854093-94 (fax: +92 (51) 2256-INN(466)). Starting around Pak Rs 3,000/night.

- ✓ Crown Plaza, 99-E Jinnah Avenue, Blue Area (near Citibank and Zero-poin), +92 (51) 227-7890. 4-star range hotel (not related to the Crowne Plaza chain) around Rs9000/night.

- ✓ Envoy Continental Hotel, 111-F Fazal-e-Haq Road, Blue Area (near Clinc Chowk), +92 (51) 227391-7. checkout: 12:00pm. 3-star range hotel, nice rooftop restaurant, internet center and phone center. around Rs3,500/night.

- ✓ Paramid II Guest House, House # 248, Street # 31,G-8/2 (Near Tipu Market), +92-300-8525521. checkin: 1300 HRS; checkout: 1200 HRS. Economical range guesthouse with WiFi, air conditioner and heated rooms. PKR 1800-2800/night.

- ✓ Rooms Islamabad, Street 50, Rohtas Road, G-9/1, +92 (364) 4912278 (roomsislamabad@gmail.com). 4-star range Guest House with in-room LCD TVs, satellite channels, powerbackup, and WiFi, available to let on daily, weekly and monthly basis. Starting from 2,000PKR per night.

- ✓ Sabipak Travelers Home Hotel & Guest Houses Network Pakistan (Dreams Hospitality), House No. 21, Street No. 38, Sector F-6/1, +92 (0)300-5192413 (sabipak@gmail.com). Affordable rooms. around PKR 2200/night.

Splurge
- ✓ The Riviera, House 5 , F-8/1. +92 (0) 51 2816157. "The Riviera", a Corporate only

premium service guest house and business centre located in the heart of the city.

✓ Serena Hotel, Khayaban-e-Suhrawardy, F-6. +92 (0) 51 111-133133. This 5-star hotel is the nicest in the city, with great restaurants and a gym. Rooms and suites $300-700. Presidential suite $2000.

✓ Number Three, 3 College Road, F-7/3. +92 (0) 51 2822070 -71. A boutique hotel in a posh residential area, with private terraces and stunning views of the Margalla Hills.

✓ Number Three Lush, House 27-A, Street 18, F-7/2. +92 (0) 51 2651070 – 72. A boutique hotel in a posh residential area, with a restaurant and business center.

✓ Marriott Hotel, Agha Khan Road, Shalimar 5. +92 (0) 51 111-223344. Ravaged by a truck bomb in September 2008, it's once again open for business, with much tighter security. Second only to the Serena Hotel, but with higher food sanitation standards.

- ✓ Embassy Lodge, Club Road (close to Rawal Lake). A comfortable and safe place with good service.

- ✓ Islamabad Club, a fine and prestigious place to stay. Reservation required and only for members and their guests.

Forthcoming luxury hotels that may or may not be built:

- ✓ Centaurus hotel and convention centre. Jinnah Avenue, Sector F-8. 7 star hotel with convention centre, mega mall and many other amenities.

- ✓ Grand Hyatt tower and apartments. Constitution Avenue.

- ✓ LE MERIDIAN hotel, another luxurious hotel under construction.
- ✓ Jumeirah hotel, 7 star hotel in capital.
- ✓ Sheraton hotel and country club, Bahria town, a luxurious hotel that will likely never be completed. There is a good, and functional, restaurant on site, with great views of the golf course, which is in operation. 1200 rupees for 9 holes of golf.
- ✓ Sunset Motel and BBQ, Only 7 Km From Islamabad International Airport, Executive rooms and suites for the discerning officials, business and leisure travlers are designed to provide every luxury for a relaxing yet productive stay ensuring the very best value for your money

Contact

The area code for Islamabad is 51. To dial from within pakistan, dial 051-xxx-xxxx

The Police emergency number is 15. There are various Police stations in the city with staff available 24/7.

Embassies
- ✓ Embassy of the Federal Republic of Germany, Ramna 5, Diplomatic Enclave/P.O. box 1027,Islamabad, +92-51 227 9441 (visa) or +92-51 2279 430-35 (emergencies) (fax: +92-51 2279 436). Mondays to Thursdays from 08:00 to 13:00 and 13:30-15:00, Fridays 08:00-13:30.
- ✓ Embassy of the Hellenic Republic Greece, 33A, School Road, F-6/2, 44000, Islamabad, +92-51 282 5186, Emergencies:+92 303 519

3105 (gremb.isl@mfa.gr, fax: +92-51 282 5161).

✓ High Commission of Malaysia, Plot No. 144-150 Street No. 17 Sector G-5, Diplomatic Enclave Islamabad, +92 51 207 2900 Emergencies for Malaysian citizens only :+92 302 844 3021 (fax: +92-51 283 3210). Monday to Friday from 08:00 to 17:00.

Stay safe

Islamabad is generally a safe and calm city. The security forces seem to have put a lid on things, and the city has been calm since the beginning of 2010 with very few bombings, shootings and kidnappings. There was an explosion at a fruit market in the outskirts on 9 April 2014 and terrorists attacked a court in the F8 on 3 March 2014. However Islamabad is clearly safer than other Pakistani cities like Peshawar.

The police have set up numerous checkpoints on roads to sensitive buildings and on the roads entering the city. These are usually harmless and they'll wave you through, but to access Constitution Avenue (inc the Serena hotel) the police will want to look in the boot of your car. If you are travelling with alcohol, make sure you have the required documents with you (like a foreign passport), as the police will try to extract a bribe from you otherwise. This rule obviously does not apply to official cars with diplomatic immunity, which the police cannot do anything about.

While travelling in city, you should keep your national identity card, passport, or driving license with you to prove your identity.

Crime-wise Islamabad is safe. Men can walk pretty much anywhere in the city day or night with little to fear. Lone women will attract male attention, particularly in areas of the city not often frequented by westerners. In those cases, its good to be in a group, and avoid dimly lit streets. But that rule applies to all cities. Also there is a rapidly growing wealthy Chinese diaspora in Islamabad, so locals are now more used to seeing foreigners around.

The Red Mosque in G6 and immediate surrounds aren't recommended given the history attached to this area.

Stay healthy

Bottled water is a good idea. Although water in Islamabad is generally clean, it is mainly gained from mountain water and tube wells and may contain minerals your system is not used to, and may not be stored and carried in the cleanest of ways. At your hotel, don't rely on them to provide you with bottled water, as many budget hotels reuse old bottles with tap water, to save money. Buy them directly from your local grocery store

Most locals do not drink tap water, but may get water from Govt. installed filteration plans. Tap water is normally boiled and it is strongly suggested that you carry bottled water and request it at all food places. Also make sure the seal is intact. If you are unsure about the hygiene of a particular place, try to avoid ice in all your drinks.

Healthcare is cheap in Pakistan, and does not require insurance. There are 3 major hospitals in

Islamabad. Pakistan Institute of Medical Sciences also known as PIMS next to G-8 Markaz, Shifa International Hospital in H-8/4 and Poly Clinic in sector G-6. PIMS is the most affordable out of the three, but also the busiest.

Also, there are various private hospitals in every sector in Islamabad providing extensive health care with different price ranges. Ali Medical Centre in F-8 Markaz is one of them.

Blue Area and Super Market (F-6) both have the two most trusted names in drug stores, Shaheen Chemists and D. Watson. Both the stores are reliable and will be able to offer sound advice for minor ailments. They also carry a wide variety of European and American foods, albeit at a high price. They may even have a doctor at the facility, should a quick suggestion be required.

Both these stores also offer Optician services and can make prescription glasses and lenses for you.

Dental care in Islamabad, is also readily available, just very expensive. Expect to pay around Rs. 10,000 ($100) for each dental cavity. Rahman & Rahman Dental Surgeons, Malik Dental Associates, and Z Dental Studio, are all good options.

Respect
Although Islamabad may look relatively modern, superficially hinting at a Western lifestyle, there are some basic guidelines to keep in mind given the cutural values of Pakistan's society:

- ✓ People are very friendly and indeed very good hosts. Many of Islamabad's citizens are well-educated and speak English very well, working for the government and in the private sector.

✓ Generally, women do not shake hands with men, though this varies greatly by social class, social setting, age and personal upbringing. A good rule of thumb for both men and women: do not shake hands with members of the opposite sex unless they extend their hands first (in which case it would be rude of you not to shake hands). The best way to greet someone is to nod and say "Assalam-u-alaikum:" smiling always helps!

✓ Don't consume alcohol in public.

✓ It's a good idea to avoid taking photographs of military establishments, police stations and anyone in uniform (army officers wear khaki, naval officers wear white, and the

Islamabad police wear navy blue trousers with a light blue shirt). If in doubt, permission can be requested from the officers concerned.

✓ Islamabad is relatively safe, compared to other Pakistani cities, or indeed most other capital cities: violent crime is very rare, but use precautions as you would in any other city.

Media
Newspapers
English Local Newspaper The Dawn, The News, The Express Tribune, The Nation & The Daily Times are national newspapers in English supplemented with local news sections.

Business Recorder is the only newpaper providing national and international business news. However, newspapers like International

Herald Tribune, Financial Times, Khaleej Times, Gulf News, Sunday Times and etc., are also available. These international newspapers usually arrive in Islamabad a day after publishing.

All newspapers (international, national and local) are available at book stores in leading hotels like Serena & Marriott. They can also be purchased from leading book stores such as London Book House (Kohsar Market in sector F-6/3), Saeed Book Bank (Jinnah Super Market in sector F-7), and Mr. Books (Super Market in sector F-6).

Discover
Islamabad is well situated for day trips and weekend trips to nearby cities and attractions.

Day trips

- ✓ Rawalpindi

- ✓ Taxila, an ancient Buddhist and Hindu site with strong Greek influence from Alexander the Great's time. Worth a visit and a picnic. Should you be interested further in the subject, guided tours can be arranged for sites around the museum.

- ✓ Murree & the Galis, One hour scenic journey through beautiful mountains to the hill resort of Murree which is a nice place to visit especially during the summer. A small place has a weather entirely different to that of Islamabad and much similar to most cities of Northern Europe. However the town is suffering under the sheer number of visitors and the small number of colonial buildings have been swamped by a plethora of cheap hotels and consequently many visitors feel the town does not live up to its guidebook hype. Chairlifts of Murree and Patriata, Kashmir point are attractions for tourists. A two kilometer "Mall" is the center of gravity of Murree where all the shops and hotels are located. If you want to escape the crowds head further north towards Nathia Gali where there are several small towns with easy access to the mountains. If driving to Murree be aware that the roads are very winding and busy and not fun to drive in the dark. Driving through Murree is also not much fun.

✓ Simly Dam It is situated at a distance of about 30 km east of Islamabad (look for the route on Google maps). A very picturesque lake spread over an area of 28,750 acres. There is not much there, some walking trails to the side of the lake (not possible to do a full circuit) and there is a guesthouse / lodge / cafe place on the dam itself. This isn't a place many Islamabad dwellers visit, and can be eerily quiet best not to visit alone.

- ✓ Rawat Fort and the Mankiala Stupa to the south of Rawalpindi can fill an afternoon
- ✓ Khan Pur Lake a 1 hour drive north-west of the city.
- ✓ Kallar Kahar lake is 2 hours down the motorway can go boating on the lake and visit some pleasant nearby shrines.
- ✓ Ketas Temples and the Khewra Salt mines makes for a pleasant day trip the Salt Mines are good to visit in the summer as a place to escape the punishing heat of the salt range. The road between Ketas and Khewra is also spectacular.

- ✓ Malot temple in the Salt Range makes for an off-the-beaten-track destination about a 2 hour drive from Islamabad down the motorway. Coordinates are 32.684537° N 72.799391° E. You need to drive through the Lafarge cement factory to get there the vista is as spectacular as the temple and a nice spot for a picnic.

- ✓ Chiniot is an oft overlooked gem located just off the motorway near Faisalabad (about a 3 hour drive). Interesting old town and a centre for wooden furniture manufacture (hence a great place to go if you are furnishing a house). The Umar Hayat Palace is quite amazing also.

- ✓ Rohtas Fort 2 hour drive south of Islamabad off the GT road enormous old fort that makes for a great day trip from Islamabad. Leave the old water well until last.

✓ Peshawar can be visited in a long day trip about 2.5 hours on the motorway visit the museum, have lunch, then go for a guided wander around the old town before heading back to Islamabad. May not be safe for Westerners.

Weekend trips

✓ Lahore makes a great weekend destination although you'll need more than 2 days to see everything. Gets very hot in the summer however so this makes a good winter weekend break.

✓ Combine a trip to Chiniot and Faisalabad spending a day in each. Staying in Kallar

Kahar (a lake halfway to Chiniot) on the Friday night is also a possibility.

✓ Perhaps a bit ambitious for a weekend but you can visit India through the Wagah border. Usually, visiting Delhi should take you half a day by car, however you will need a visa. On the way, it is advisable to see the Golden Temple in Amritsar, and many other inspiring sights.

✓ Trips to the northern mountains are possible if flying PIA flies to Chitral, Gilgit and Skardu flights can be unreliable with cancellations for poor weather / not enough passengers common. This makes a weekend trip a bit of a gamble in case your flight is cancelled and you get stuck up north. Also in a weekend there isn't enough time to get in much walking. An alternative is to drive to the which is a 6 hour drive from Islamabad and can be done in a weekend (eg leaving Friday lunchtime and overnighting in Abbottabad) but better to plan 3 or more nights if you can. Beware of landslides however if it has been raining these can easily get you stranded for a week or more best to save Kaghan for the dry season.

✓ Bishkek via Kyrgyzstan Air. Was on Friday nights around 7PM for around 340 USD one way, but this was before the Kyrg revolution. The travel agent in Islamabad, as of October 2009, is GSA Vital World Travel 9251 2274648-9 or 03125128227. airkyrgyzstan@dsl.net.pk. He accepts credit cards and is off Kulsum Plaza, Blue Area, Islamabad (flight no longer running as of 2011)

The End

Printed in Great Britain
by Amazon